Introduction

Enjoy solving a variety of mathematical pattern puzzles, including prime numbers, Fibonacci-like series, visual patterns, analogies, arrays, and more.

This book starts out easy with basic patterns and simple puzzles, and the level of difficulty steadily grows so that people of all ages and abilities can enjoy many of the patterns and puzzles in this book.

Each chapter begins with a brief introduction (and, where necessary, a quick review) of the relevant concepts, followed by 2-3 examples of pattern puzzles with explanations.

The answer, along with an explanation, to every puzzle can be found at the end of the book.

Some chapters incorporate ideas from earlier chapters. For example, once prime numbers are introduced in Chapter 8 and the Fibonacci sequence is introduced in Chapter 9, these concepts may appear in a subsequent chapter.

Examples

Following are a few examples of the kinds of patterns that you can find in this book. Fill in the blanks.

Example 1.

9, 25, 49, 81, _121_, _169_, _225_, _289_

Example 2.

15, 15, 10, 30, 30, 20, 60, 60, 40, _120_, _120_, _80_

Example 3.

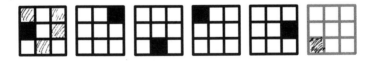

Check your answers on the next page.

300+

Mathematical
Pattern Puzzles

Number Pattern Recognition & Reasoning

Improve Your Math Fluency Series

Chris McMullen, Ph.D.

300+ Mathematical Pattern Puzzles
Number Pattern Recognition & Reasoning

Improve Your Math Fluency Series

Chris McMullen, Ph.D.
Copyright © 2015

Cover design by Melissa Stevens
www.theillustratedauthor.net

Mathematics > Popular > Patterns
Entertainment > Puzzles > Math Games

ISBN-13: 978-1512044287
ISBN-10: 1512044288

www.chrismcmullen.com
www.improveyourmathfluency.com

IMPROVE FLUENCY

YOUR MATH

Contents

Answer to Example 1.

Square odd numbers: $3 \times 3 = 9$, $5 \times 5 = 25$, $7 \times 7 = 49$, and $9 \times 9 = 81$. The next four numbers are $11 \times 11 = 121$, $13 \times 13 = 169$, $15 \times 15 = 225$, and $17 \times 17 = 289$.

Answer to Example 2.

The first 3 numbers are 15, 15, and 10. Double these to get 30, 30, and 20. Double those to get 60, 60, and 40. The next three numbers are 120, 120, and 80.

Answer to Example 3.

The black square advances 3 spaces clockwise along the large square:

1 Ordered

The patterns in Chapter 1 follow a common recognizable order, like whole numbers (1, 2, 3, 4, 5...), the alphabet (a, b, c, d, e...), or geometric shapes (triangle, square, pentagon, hexagon, heptagon...).

Example 1. These even numbers progress in order, beginning with 6.

6, 8, 10, 12, 14, 16, 18...

The next two numbers are 20 and 22.

Example 2. These letters of the alphabet appear in order, skipping every other letter, beginning with m.

m, o, q, s, u...

It's really m, skip n, o, skip p, q, skip r, s,

skip t, u, skip v. The next two letters are w and y (since x is skipped).

Example 3. This visual pattern consists of polygons. Count the number of sides. The triangle has 3 sides, the square has 4 sides, the pentagon has 5 sides, etc.

The next two shapes are an octagon (8 sides) and nonagon (9 sides):

#1
    7, _9_, 11, _13_, _15_, 17, 19, _21_

#2
    5, _10_, 15, _20_, _25_, 30, _35_, 40

#3
_500_, 600, 700, _800_, 900, _1000_, _1100_, 1200

#4
    25, 50, _75_, _100_, 125, _150_, 175, _200_

#5

_53_, 65, 77, _89_, _101_, 113, _125_, 137

#6

b, d, f, _h_, j, _l_, _n_, p

#7

c, g, k, _o_, s, _w_

#8

square | octagon

_____, _____, _____, ,

#9

#10

15, _14_, 13, _12_, 11, _10_, _9_, 8

#11

_30_, 27, 24, 21, _18_, 15, _12_, _9_

#12

125, _120_, 115, _110_, _105_, 100, _95_, 90

#13

1100, 1075, 1050, 1025, 1000, 975, 950, 925

#14

x, w, v, u, t, s, r, q

#15

q, o, m, k, i, g, e, c

#16

y, v, s, p, m, j, g, d

#17

#18

#19

A, E, I, O, U

3 3 5 5

#20

d, f, g, h, i, k, l, m, n, p, q

2 Patterned

The sequences of Chapter 2 follow a repeating pattern. For example, 1, 7, 5, 1, 7, 5, 1, 7, 5 repeats the digits 1, 7, and 5.

Example 1. These digits alternate: five, then three, five again, then three again.

$$5, 3, 5, 3, 5, 3, 5...$$

The next two numbers are 3 and 5.

Example 2. These letters follow a pattern: 1 Q, then 2 E's, 1 Q, 2 E's, 1 Q, 2E's, etc.

$$Q, E, E, Q, E, E, Q, E, E, Q...$$

The next two letters are E and E.

Example 3. This pattern grows. Each number gains one digit in order. The number 9 turns into 98, then 987, followed by 9876, and so on.

9, 98, 987, 9876, 98765, 987654...

The next two numbers are 9876543 and 98765432.

#1

0, 1, 0, 1, 0, _1_, _0_, _1_

#2

t, _y_, _t_, _y_, t, y, t, y

#3

A, a, _A_, a, A, a, A, a, _A_, _a_

#4

2, 4, 8, 2, 4, 8, 2, _4_, _8_, _2_

#5

z, x, q, z, x, q, z, x, _q_, _z_, _x_

#6

♡, ✷, ☽, ♡, ✷, ☽, ♡, ✷, ☽, ♡

#7

9, 9, 4, 9, 9, 4, 9, _9_, _4_, _9_

#8

3, 5, 3, 3, 5, 3, 3, _5_, _3_, _3_

#9

G, g, g, G, g, g, _G_, _g_, _g_, G

#10

F, F, e, F, _F_, e, F, F, _e_, _F_

#11

☺, ☹, ☺, ☺, ☹, ☺, ☺, _☹_, _☺_, _☺_

#12

2, 5, 3, 9, 2, 5, 3, 9, 2, 5, _3_, _9_, _2_

#13

1, 7, 6, 4, 8, 1, 7, 6, 4, 8, 1, 7, 6, _4_, _8_, _1_

#14

D, b, P, q, D, b, P, q, D, b, P, _q_, _D_, _b_

#15

C, e, H, j, c, E, h, J, C, e, H, _j_, _c_, _E_

#16

8, 2, 8, 8, 2, 8, 8, 8, 2, 8, 8, 8, 8,

2, 8, 8, 8, _8_ , _8_ , _2_

#17

6, _77_ , 888, _9999_ , 1010101010,

111111111111, 12121212121212,

_1313131313131313_

#18

2, 23, 234, 2345, _23456_ , _234567_ , _2345678_

#19

1, 31, _531_ , 7531, 97531,

1197531, _131197531_ , _15131197531_

#20

4, 4, 3, 12, 12, 9, 36, 36, 27, _108_, _108_ , _81_, _324_

3 Alternating

An alternating sequence has two (or more) patterns intertwined. For example, consider the two patterns 1, 2, 3, 4... and A, B, C, D... They can be combined together in a single alternating pattern like 1, A, 2, B, 3, C, 4, D...

Example 1. This pattern alternately merges one sequence of odd numbers with another sequence consisting of every other letter of the alphabet. One pattern is 1, 3, 5, 7, 9, 11, 13... The second pattern is b, d, f, h, j, l, n... See how these merge together below.

$$1, b, 3, d, 5, f, 7, h, 9, j, 11, l...$$

The next two elements are 13 (following 11) and n (following the letter l).

Example 2. The first pattern of this alternating sequence counts by four: 4, 8, 12, 16, 20... The second pattern subtracts three: 36, 33, 30, 27, 24...

4, 36, 8, 33, 12, 30, 16, 27, 20, 24...

The next two numbers are 24 (adding 4 to 20) and 21 (subtracting 3 from the previous 24).

Example 3. Both of these patterns consist of letters. The first has letters progressing forward: A, B, C, D, E... The second has letters going backward: M, L, K, J, I...

A, M, B, L, C, K, D, J, E, I...

The next two letters are F (coming after E) and H (coming before I).

#1

11, 99, 22, 88, <u>33</u>, <u>77</u>, 44, 66, <u>55</u>, <u>55</u>, 66, 44

#2

3, 18, 6, 16, 9, 14, 12, 12, <u>15</u>, <u>10</u>, <u>18</u>, <u>8</u>

#3

6, 24, 12, <u>24</u>, <u>18</u>, 24, 24, 24, 30, <u>24</u>, <u>36</u>

#4

5, 6, 7, 9, 9, 12, 11, 15, <u>13</u>, <u>18</u>, <u>15</u>, <u>21</u>

#5

10, 50, 15, 40, 20, 30, 25, <u>20</u>, <u>30</u>, <u>10</u>, <u>35</u>

#6

p, q, o, r, n, s, m, <u>t</u>, <u>l</u>, <u>u</u>, <u>k</u>

#7

<u>Z</u>, <u>N</u>, <u>X</u>, <u>O</u>, V, P, T, Q, R, R, P

#8

c, f, d, <u>f</u>, <u>e</u>, f, f, f, g, f, h, <u>f</u>, <u>i</u>

#9

J, 29, L, 26, N, 23, P, 20, <u>R</u>, <u>17</u>, <u>T</u>, <u>14</u>

#10

7, z, <u>11</u>, <u>w</u>, 15, t, 19, <u>q</u>, <u>13</u>, n

#11

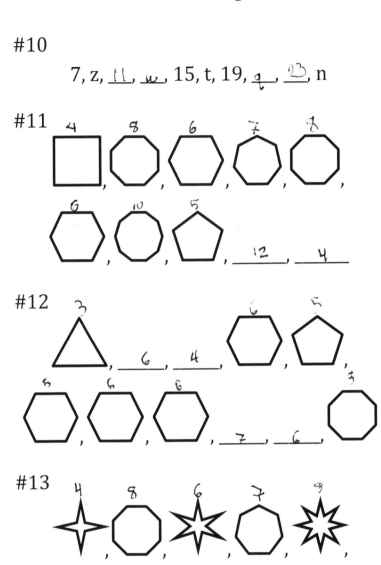

#12

#13

#14

→, ↑, ↓, ↓, ←, ↑, ↑, ↓, →, ↑, ↓, ↓, ←, ↑

#15

↑, ←, ←, ↖, ↓, ↑, →, ↗, ↑, →, ←, ↘, ↓, ↓

#16

Q, z, X, w, Q, z, X, w, Q, z, X, w, Q

#17

1, 0, 0, 0, 1, 1, 0, 0, 1, 0, 0, 1, 1,

0, 0, 0, 1, 1, 0, 0, 1, 0, 0, 1

#18

D, e, f, F, H, g, j, H, L, i, n, J, P, k, r

#19

30, 70, 25, 35, 60, 35, 40, 50, 45, 45,

40, 55, 50, 30, 65, 55, 20, 75, 60, 10

#20

K, h, Q, L, i, P, M, j, O, N, k,

N, O, l, M, P, m, L, Q, n

4 Cyclic

A pattern that repeats itself in some way is cyclic. For example, time is cyclic. The hours vary from 1 to 12 and then start over again at 1. That is, after 12 o'clock comes 1 o'clock.

Example 1. These 3 digits cycle in the same order repeatedly: 418, then 184, and then 841.

$$418, 184, 841, 418, 184, 841...$$

The next two numbers are 418 and 184.

Example 2. The single-digit odd numbers are cyclic, where after 9 we continue again with 1.

$$1, 3, 5, 7, 9, 1, 3, 5...$$

The next two numbers are 7 and 9.

Example 3. This pattern continues in half hour increments of time.

10:00, 10:30, 11:00, 11:30,
12:00, 12:30, 1:00, 1:30...

The next two times are 2:00 and 2:30.

#1
927, 279, 792, 927, 279, _792_, _923_, _279_, _792_

#2
3841, 8413, 4138, 1384, 3841,

_8413_ , _4138_ , _1384_ , _3841_

#3
4, 6, 8, 0, 2, 4, 6, _8̶0̶_, _0_ , _2_ , _4_

#4
_7_, 88, _999_, 0000, 11111,

222222, _3333333_ , _444444444_

#5
123, 132, 231, _213_, _312_,

321, 123, 132, _231_ , _213_

#6

act, cta, tac, act, cta, _tac_, _act_, _cta_, _tac_

#7

spot, _pots_, _otsp_, tspo,

spot, pots, _otsp_, _tspo_

#8

u, w, _y_, _a_, c, _e_, g, _i_, k

#9

ccccccccc, bbbbbbbb, _aaaaaaa_, _zzzzzz_,

yyyyy, _xxxx_, www, _vv_

#10

Roygbiv, rOygbiv, _roYgbiv_,

royGbiv, _roygBiv_, _roygbIv_,

roygbiV, Roygbiv, _rOygbiv_

#11

0, 11, _222_, 3333, 222,

_11_, 0, 11, _222_, 3333, _222_

#12

CIRCLE, IRCLEC, RCLECI, CLECIR,

LECIRC, ECIRCL, CIRCLE, IRCLEC, RCLECI

#13

10:45, 11:15, 11:45, 12:15,

12:45, 1:15, 1:45, 2:15

#14

9:30, 10:15, 11:00, 11:45,

12:30, 1:15, 2:00, 2:45

#15

Friday, Saturday, Sunday, Monday,

Tuesday, Wednesday, Thursday, Friday

#16

October, November, December, January,

February, March, April, May

#17

north, _____east_____, south, west, north,

_____east_____, _____south_____, _____west_____

#18

east, northeast, north,

_____northwest_____, west, southwest, _____south_____,

southeast, _____east_____, _____northeast_____

#19

north, southeast, west,

northeast, south, northwest,

_____east_____, _____southwest_____ _____north_____, _____southeast_____

#20

90°, 180°, 270°, 360°, 90°,

_____180°_____, _____270°_____, _____360°_____, _____90°_____

5 Additive & Multiplicative

The patterns of Chapter 5 involve one of the four basic arithmetic operations: addition, subtraction, multiplication, or division. (However, the operations are not merged together until Chapter 6.)

Example 1. This sequence is made by adding 4 repeatedly, beginning with 5.

$$5, 9, 13, 17, 21, 25, 29...$$

The next two numbers are 33 and 37.

Example 2. This pattern involves multiplying the previous answer by 2.

$$3, 6, 12, 24, 48...$$

The next two numbers are 96 and 192.

Example 3. This sequence is made by subtracting 8 each time.

70, 62, 54, 46, 38, 30, 22...

The next two numbers are 14 and 6.

#1

6, 12, 18, 24, _30_, _36_, _42_, _48_

#2

72, 64, 56, 48, _40_, _32_, _24_, _16_

#3

_1_, _2_, 4, 8, 16, 32, _64_, _128_

#4

7, 13, _19_, _25_, 31, 37, _43_, _49_

#5

640, 320, 160, 80, _40_, _20_, _10_, _5_

#6

_33_, 37, 41, _45_, _49_, 53, 57, _61_

#7

_52_, _45_, 38, 31, _24_, 17, 10, _3_

#8

25, _50_, _100_, _200_, _400_, 800, 1600, 3200

#9

6, _11_, 16, _21_, 26, _31_, 36, _41_

#10

_1_, 20, _39_, 58, _77_, 96, _115_, 134

#11

9, 18, _27_, _36_, 45, _54_, 63, _72_

#12

_46_, 40, 34, 28, _22_, _16_, 10, _4_

#13

8, 16, _32_, 64, _128_, _256_, 512, ____

#14

_9_, 21, 33, _45_, 57, 69, _81_, _93_

#15

768, 384, 192, 96, _48_, _24_, _12_, _6_

#16

212, _199_, 186, 173, _160_, 147, _134_, _121_

#17

____2____, ____6____, 18, ___54___, 162, 486, 1458, __4374__

#18

162
4
1048

192, __316__, __240__, 264, 288, 312, ____, ____

#19

____2____, __10__, 50, 250, 1250, 6250, _31250_, _156250_

#20

2187, 729, 243, 81, __27__, __9__, __3__, __1__

6 Multiple Operations

Multiple arithmetic operations (addition, subtraction, multiplication, and division) are merged together in these sequences. For example, the same sequence may involve both addition and multiplication.

Example 1. This sequence involves multiplying the previous term by 2 and then adding 1. For example, $2 \times 3 + 1 = 7$ and $2 \times 7 + 1 = 15$.

$$3, 7, 15, 31, 63, 127...$$

The next two numbers are 255 (because $2 \times 127 + 1 = 255$) and 511 (since $2 \times 255 + 1 = 511$).

Note that you can also make this pattern

by adding 4, then adding 8, then adding 16, then adding 32, each time adding twice as much as previously: $3 + 4 = 7$, $7 + 8 = 15$, $15 + 16 = 31$, $31 + 32 = 63...$

Example 2. This pattern is made by adding 2, then adding 3, then adding 2, then adding 3, continuing to alternate. For example, $4 + 2 = 6$, $6 + 3 = 9$, $9 + 2 = 11$, and $11 + 3 = 14$.

$$4, 6, 9, 11, 14, 16, 19...$$

The next two numbers are 21 (since $19 + 2 = 21$) and 24 (since $21 + 3 = 24$).

Example 3. This sequence is made by alternately multiplying by 2 and dividing by 3. Beginning with 324, multiplying by 2 makes 648, dividing by 3 makes 216, multiplying by 2 makes 432, dividing by 3 makes 144, and so on.

$$324, 648, 216, 432, 144...$$

The next two numbers are 288 (since 144 × 2 = 288) and 96 (since 288 / 3 = 96). (Note that the slash can be used for division: 288 / 3 = 288 ÷ 3 = 96.)

#1

2, 7, 22, 67, 202, _607_, _1822_, _5467_, _16402_

#2

3, 9, 8, 14, 13, 19, 18, _24_, _23_, _29_, _28_

#3

1022, 510, 254, 126, 62, _30_, _14_, _6_, _2_

#4

1, 3, 6, 18, 36, 108,

216, _648_, _1296_, _3888_, _6776_

#5

101, 99, 95, 93, 89, _87_, _83_, _81_, _77_

#6

÷2   +16   ÷2   +16   ÷2
256, 128, 144, 72, 88, 44,

+16
60, _30_, _46_, _23_, _39_

#7

3, 5, 9, _17_, 33, _65_, _129_, 257, _503_

#8

5, 7, 15, 17, 35, 37, 75, 77,

155, _157_, _165_, _163_ _173_

#9

1, 3, 6, 10, 15, 21, _28_, _36_, _45_, _55_

#10

4, 6, 9, 13, 18, 24, _31_, _39_, _48_, _58_

#11

100, 51, 98, 53, 95, 56, 91,

60, _86_, _65_, _80_, _71_

#12

8, 4, 12, 6, 24, 12, 60, 30, 180, 90,

630, _315_, _2520_, _1260_, _1340_

#13

50, 52, 47, 55, 43, 59, 38,

64, 32, _70_, _25_, _77_, _17_

#14

10, 50, 20, 100, 70, 350, 320,

1600, _1570_, _7850_, _7820_, _39100_

#15

1, 3, 6, 9, 18, 22, 44, 49,

98, _104_, _208_, _215_, _430_

#16

2, 2, 1, 2, 1, 3, 2, 8, 7, 35,

34, _204_, _203_, _1421_, _1420_

#17

a, d, c, f, e, h, g, j, i, l, k, _n_, _m_, _p_, _o_

#18

1, 2, 6, 9, 10, 14, 17, 18, 22, 25, 26,

30, 33, _34_, _38_, _41_, _42_

#19

2, 5, 10, 9, 12, 24, 23, 26, 52, 51, 54,

+3 ·2 −1 ·3 ·2 −1 +3 ·2 −1 ·3

108, 107, _110_, _220_, _219_, _222_

−1 +3 ·2 −1 +3

#20

8, 6, 24, 12, 10, 40, 20, 18, 72, 36, 34,

−2 ·4 ÷2 −2 ·4 ÷2 −2 ·4 ÷2 −2

136, 68, _66_, _264_, _132_, _130_

÷2 −2 ·4 ÷2 −2

7 Digits

Each sequence in Chapter 7 involves changing one or more digits of a multi-digit number. For example, the number 384 has three digits: The hundreds digit is 3, the tens digit is 8, and the units digit is 4. A possible pattern is to raise the hundreds digit by 1 and reduce the tens digit by 2. If so, the next number would be 464 (since 3 + 1 = 4 and 8 – 2 = 6), followed by 544 (since 4 + 1 = 5 and 6 – 2 = 4).

Example 1. In this sequence of three-digit numbers, the first digit decreases, the second digit remains unchanged, and the third digit increases. For example, 951 becomes 852 as the 9 decreases to 8 and the 1 increases to 2. Watch how the first digit changes from 8, 7, 6..., the middle digit is always 5, and the last digit changes from 1, 2, 3...

951, 852, 753, 654, 555...

The next two numbers are 456 and 357.

Example 2. The digits in this sequence cycle through a pattern. They rearrange themselves in order.

123, 132, 213, 231, 312...

The next two numbers are 321 and 123.

Example 3. In this sequence, the digits add up to 9. As examples, look at 63, where $6 + 3 = 9$, and 108, where $1 + 0 + 8 = 9$.

63, 72, 81, 90, 108, 117...

The next two numbers are 126 and 135.

(Note that the digits of 99 add up to 18.

Although the 1 and 8 of 18 add up to 9, this example is only counting the first sum of the digits, which is why 99 is skipped.)

#1

807, 716, 625, 534, 443, 352, 261, 170

#2

29, 47, 65, 83, 21, 49, 67, 85, 23, 41

#3

122, 223, 324, 425, 526, 627, 728, 829

#4

369, 396, _____, 693, 936,

_____, 369, _____, _____

#5

5678, 5687, 5768, 5786, _____, 5876,

6578, _____, 6758, _____, _____, 6875

#6

3456, 3465, _____, 5463, 6435,

6453, 3456, _____, _____, _____

#7

d8, f7, h6, j5, ___, ___, ___, ___

#8

y3C, v5d, s7E, p9f, m1G,

_____, _____, _____, _____

#9

T8e2, r7Q4, P6E6, n5q8, L4e0,

j3Q2, _____, _____, _____, _____

#10

24680, 24681, 24691, 24791,

25791, 35791, 35792, 35702,

_____, _____, _____, _____

#11

89, 98, 179, 188, 197, 269,

278, _____, _____, _____, _____

#12
10, 11, 20, 12, 21, 30, 13, ____, ____, ____, ____

#13
39, 57, 75, 93, 1119, _____, 1155, 1173,

1191, 1317, _____, _____, _____

#14

117, 144, 171, 225, 252, 333,

414, _____, _____, _____, 1116, _____

#15

13, 35, 57, 79, 135, 357,

579, _____, _____, _____

#16

892, 128, 783, 237, 674, 346,

565, 455, _____, _____, _____, _____

#17

    _____, Atc, _____, Cta, Tac,

    Tca, _____, Atc, _____, Cta

#18

    _____, TOSP, TPOS, TPSO, TSOP, _____,

SOPT, SOTP, _____, SPTO, _____, STPO

#19

    bit, diq, fin, hik, jih, _____,

    _____, piy, _____, _____, vip

#20

    Ae, Bd, Cc, Db, Ea, Aad,

    Abc, _____, _____, _____, _____

#21

  123, 342, 534, 456, 675, 867, 789, 908,

190, 012, 231, _____, _____, _____, _____

8 Prime Numbers

A prime number is a positive integer that is evenly divisible only by itself and the number one. For example, 7 is prime because it can only be factored as 7 × 1, while 6 is not prime because it can be factored as 2 × 3 in addition to 6 × 1.

The first several prime numbers are:

2, 3, 5, 7, 11, 13, 17, 19, 23, 29, 31...

Example 1. This sequence is formed by skipping every other prime number starting with 5. The pattern is 5, skip 7, 11, skip 13, 17, skip 19, 23, skip 29, 31, etc.

5, 11, 17, 23, 31...

The next two numbers are 41 and 47

(since 37 and 43 are skipped).

Example 2. This pattern doubles each prime number. For example, $2 \times 2 = 4$, $2 \times 3 = 6$, and $2 \times 5 = 10$.

$$4, 6, 10, 14, 22...$$

The next two numbers are 26 (since $2 \times 13 = 26$) and 34 (since $2 \times 17 = 34$).

#1

29, 31, 37, 41, 43, _47_, _51_, _53_, _59_

#2

4, 6, 8, 9, 10, 12, 14, 15, _16_, _18_, _20_, _21_

#3

_93_, 89, _84_, 79, _75_, 71, _66_, 61

#4

2, 3, 7, 11, 17, 19, 29,

31, 41, _43_, _51_, _53_, _61_

#5

    3, 4, 6, 8, 12, 14, _18_ , _20_ , _24_ , _30_

#6

    11, 31, 41, 61, 71, _91_ , _101_ , _121_ , _131_

#7

    3, 5, 7, 23, 29, 41, 43,

    47, ____, ____, ____, ____, 113

#8

9, 21, 39, 57, 87, 111, _129_ , _153_ , _177_ , _201_

#9

21, 25, 33, 37, 45, 57, 61, ____, ____, ____, ____

#10

    4, 10, 22, 34, 46, 62, ____, ____, ____, ____

#11

    101, 103, 107, 109, 113,

    ____, ____, ____, ____

#12

102, 103, 105, 107, 111,

113, ____, ____, ____, ____

#13

3, 5, 5, 7, 11, 13, 17, 19, 29,

31, 41, 43, ____, ____, ____, ____

#14

2, 3, 5, 7, 11, 23, 29, 41, 43,

47, 61, 67, 83, ____, ____, ____, ____

9 Fibonacci Inspired

The Fibonacci sequence adds consecutive terms together. The Fibonacci sequence begins with 0 and 1, adds these together to make 1, then $1 + 1$ makes 2, followed by $1 + 2 = 3, 2 + 3 = 5, 3 + 5 = 8, 5 + 8 = 13$, and so on.

The patterns in Chapter 9 are not necessarily the Fibonacci sequence itself, but they do involve performing arithmetic operations (addition, subtraction, multiplication, or division) on the previous terms. In this way, these patterns are Fibonacci-inspired.

Example 1. The Fibonacci sequence begins with 0, 1, and then adds the two previous elements together to make the next element. As examples, $0 + 1 = 1$, $1 + 1 = 2, 1 + 2 = 3, 2 + 3 = 5, 3 + 5 = 8$, and $5 + 8 = 13$.

$$0, 1, 1, 2, 3, 5, 8, 13, 21, 34...$$

The next two numbers are 55 (since $21 + 34 = 55$) and 89 (since $34 + 55 = 89$).

Example 2. This sequence multiplies the previous two numbers instead of adding them. For example, $2 \times 3 = 6$ and $3 \times 6 = 18$.

$$2, 3, 6, 18, 108...$$

The next two numbers are 1944 (since $18 \times 108 = 1944$) and 209952 (since $108 \times 1944 = 209952$).

Example 3. This sequence is similar to the Fibonacci sequence except that it adds the last 3 numbers rather than the last 2. For example, $0 + 1 + 2 = 3, 1 + 2 + 3 = 6$, and $2 + 3 + 6 = 11$.

$$0, 1, 2, 3, 6, 11, 20, 37...$$

The next two numbers are 68 (since $11 + 20 + 37 = 68$) and 125 (since $20 + 37 + 68 = 125$).

#1

2, 2, 4, 6, 10, 16, _26_ , _42_, _68_ , _116_

#2

_2_, 3, _4_ , 7, 11, 18, 29, 47, _76_, _123_

#3

6, _9_ , 15, _24_ , 39, 63,

_102_ , 165, _267_ , 432

#4

309, 191, 118, 73, 45,

28, _17_, _11_, _6_ , _5_

#5

1, 2, 2, 4, 8, 32, ___256___ , ___1292___ , ___330752___

256
32
5 12
7 80
1292

∞ 51 ∞

1292
256
7752
64600
25840
330752

#6

1, 2, 5, 13, 34, 89, 233, _____, _____, _____, _____

#7

1, 1, 2, 4, 7, 13, 24, 44, 81,

149, _____, _____, _____, _____

#8

2, 3, 3, 4, 5, 7, 10, 15, 23,

36, _57_, _91_, _146_, _135_

#9

1, 3, 5, 9, 15, 25, 41, 67, 109,

177, _287_, _465_, _753_, _1219_

#10

0, 1, 2, 2, 3, 5, 7, 10, 15, 22, 32, 47,

69, 101, _148_, _217_, _318_, _466_

10 Roman Numerals

This chapter involves Roman numerals. The table below provides a quick refresher of Roman numerals.

I = 1	XI = 11	L = 50
II = 2	XIV = 14	LX = 60
III = 3	XV = 15	XC = 90
IV = 4	XVI = 16	C = 100
V = 5	XIX = 19	CD = 400
VI = 6	XX = 20	D = 500
VII = 7	XXXIX = 39	CM = 900
VIII = 8	XL = 40	M = 1000
IX = 9	XLIX = 49	MM = 2000
X = 10	MMCDXLVIII = 2448	

The same symbol can appear as many as three times in a row. For example, XXX equals 30.

If a smaller symbol appears left of a larger symbol, it subtracts. For example, XL is 40 and XCV is 95 (but not VC, as X rather than V is used before C). Otherwise, smaller numbers appear to the right, in which case they add. For example, XXXIII equals 33.

As a last example of writing Roman numerals, XLV is 45, as the X subtracts 10 from 50, while the V adds 5.

Example 1. This sequence begins with Roman numeral X (ten) and counts upward by ones.

X, XI, XII, XIII, XIV, XV, XVI, XVII, XVIII...

The next two numbers are IX (nineteen) and XX (twenty).

Example 2. This pattern counts Roman numerals by fives.

V, X, XV, XX, XXV, XXX,

XXXV, XL, XLV, L, LV...

The next two numbers are LX (60) and LXV (65).

Example 3. This pattern is made by adding 2, then adding 3, then adding 2, then adding 3, continuing to alternate. For example, IV + II = VI (or 4 + 2 = 6), VI + III = IX (or 6 + 3 = 9), and IX + II = XI (or 9 + 2 = 11), and XI + III = XIV (or 11 + 3 = 14).

IV, VI, IX, XI, XIV, XVI, XIX...

The next two numbers are XXI (since 19 + 2 = 21) and XXIV (since 21 + 3 = 24).

#1

II, IV, _VI_, VIII, X, _XII_, _XIV_, XVI, _XVIII_, XX

#2

III, VI, XII, XXIV, XLVIII,

_____, _____, _____, _____

#3

CVI, CV, CIV, CIII, CII, CI,

_____, _____, _____, _____

#4

XXV, L, LXXV, C, CXXV, CL,

_____, _____, _____, _____

#5

C, CC, CCC, CD, D, DC, _____, _____, _____, _____

#6

MCMLX, MCMLXV, MCMLXX,

MCMLXXV, MCMLXXX, MCMLXXXV,

_____, _____, _____, _____

#7

DLXX, DLX, DL, DXL, DXXX, DXX,

————, ————, ————, ————

#8

IX, VII, XIV, XII, XIX, XVII, XXIV, XXII,

————, ————, ————, ————

#9

II, VI, III, IX, VI, XVIII, XV, XLV, XLII,

————, ————, ————, ————

#10

VII, IX, XII, XVI, XXI, XXVII,

————, ————, ————, ————

#11

II, IV, VI, IX, XI, XV, XX, XL, LI,

————, ————, ————, ————

#12

    CC, CD, CI, CL, CM, CV, CX, DC, DI,

_____, _____, _____, _____

#13

    III, V, IX, XVII, XXXIII, LXV, CXXIX,

_____, _____, _____, _____

#14

    I, I, II, III, V, VIII, XIII, XXI,

_____, _____, _____, _____

#15

    II, III, V, VII, XI, XIII, XVII,

_____, _____, _____, _____

11 Powers

A number raised to a power has an exponent. For example, in 3^4, the number 3 is raised to the power of 4, where 4 is called the exponent.

When a number is raised to a power, it means that the number is multiplied by itself that many times. For example, 3^4 equals $3 \times 3 \times 3 \times 3$ (four threes are multiplied together).

An exponent of 2 is called a square. For example, 5^2 is read as "five squared," and means 5×5. Thus, $5^2 = 25$.

An exponent of 3 is called a cube. For example, 2^3 is read as "two cubed," and means $2 \times 2 \times 2$. Thus, $2^3 = 8$.

Any nonzero number raised to the power

of 0 equals 1. For example, $8^0 = 1$. If you would like to know why, this is explained in Chapter 15.

Example 1. This sequence involves cubing numbers (raising them to the power of three). For example, $1^3 = 1 \times 1 \times 1 = 1$, $2^3 = 2 \times 2 \times 2 = 8$, $3^3 = 3 \times 3 \times 3 = 27$, and $4^3 = 4 \times 4 \times 4 = 64$.

$$1, 8, 27, 64, 125, 216...$$

The next two numbers are 343 (since $7^3 = 7 \times 7 \times 7 = 343$) and 512 (since $8^3 = 8 \times 8 \times 8 = 512$).

Example 2. This pattern consists of powers of three. For example, $3^0 = 1$, $3^1 = 3$, $3^2 = 3 \times 3 = 9$, $3^3 = 3 \times 3 \times 3 = 27$, and $3^4 = 3 \times 3 \times 3 \times 3 = 81$.

$$1, 3, 9, 27, 81...$$

The next two numbers are 243 (since $3^5 = 3 \times 3 \times 3 \times 3 \times 3 = 243$) and 729 (since $3^6 = 3 \times 3 \times 3 \times 3 \times 3 \times 3 = 729$).

Note that you could also make this sequence by multiplying the previous term by 3.

#1

    __1__, 4, 9, 16, __25__, 36, __49__, __64__

#2

1, __2__, __4__, 8, 16, 32, 64, __128__, __256__

#3

1, 100, 10000, 1000000, __100000000__,

__10000000000__, __1000000000000__ __100000000000000__

#4

1, 16, 81, 256, 625, 1296,

_____, _____, _____, _____

#5

4, 16, 36, 64, 100, 144,

_____, _____, _____, _____

#6

1, 4, 27, 256, 3125, _____, _____

#7

1, 16, 256, 4096, _____, _____

#8

0, 3, 8, 15, 24, 35, ____, ____, ____, ____

#9

4, 9, 25, 49, 121, 169, ____, ____, ____, ____

#10

2, 8, 18, 32, 50, 72, ____, ____, ____, ____

12 Factorials

An integer followed by an exclamation mark (!) is called a factorial. For example, 4! is read as "four factorial."

The factorial notation means to multiply the given number by successively smaller numbers until reaching the number one (except for 0! which will be explained shortly).

For example, 4! means 4 times 3 times 2 times 1, which equals $4 \times 3 \times 2 \times 1 = 24$. As another example, $3! = 3 \times 2 \times 1 = 6$. Observe that $4! = 4 \times 3!$ (since $24 = 4 \times 6$).

Note that 0! is defined to equal 1. The reason that $0! = 1$ is so that 1! can follow the rule $N! = N (N - 1)!$ for all positive integers (N > 0). This way, 1! = 1 (1 – 1)! = 0! since 1! and 0! both equal 1.

Example 1. This sequence is made from factorials. For example, 0! = 1, 1! = 1, 2! = 2 × 1 =2, 3! = 3 × 2 × 1 = 6, 4! = 4 × 3 × 2 × 1 = 24.

$$1, 1, 2, 6, 24, 120...$$

The next two numbers are 720 (since 6! = 6 × 5 × 4 × 3 × 2 × 1 = 720) and 5040 (since 7! = 7 × 6 × 5 × 4 × 3 × 2 × 1 = 5040).

Note that you could also make this pattern by multiplying the first number by 1 (1 × 1 = 1), the second number by 2 (1 × 2 = 2), the third number by 3 (2 × 3 = 6), the fourth number by 4 (6 × 4 = 24), the fifth number by 5 (24 × 5 = 120), and so on.

Example 2. The double factorial involves

just odd or even numbers. For example, $0!! = 1$, $2!! = 2$, $4!! = 4 \times 2 = 8$, $6!! = 6 \times 4 \times 2 = 48$, and $8!! = 8 \times 6 \times 4 \times 2 = 384$.

$$1, 2, 8, 48, 384, 3840...$$

The next two numbers are 46,080 (since $12!! = 12 \times 10 \times 8 \times 6 \times 4 \times 2 = 46,080$) and 645,120 (since $14!! = 14 \times 12 \times 10 \times 8 \times 6 \times 4 \times 2 = 645,120$).

Example 3. This sequence features a formula for combinations in probability. This formula is:

$$\frac{N!}{(N - M)!\, M!}$$

In this sequence, N = 8 and M grows from 0 to 8. For example,

$$\frac{8!}{(8 - 0)!\, 0!} = \frac{8!}{8!\, 0!} = 1$$

$$\frac{8!}{(8 - 1)!\, 1!} = \frac{8!}{7!\, 1!} = 8$$

$$\frac{8!}{(8-2)!\,2!} = \frac{8!}{6!\,2!} = 28$$

$$\frac{8!}{(8-3)!\,3!} = \frac{8!}{5!\,3!} = 56$$

$$\frac{8!}{(8-4)!\,4!} = \frac{8!}{4!\,4!} = 70$$

$$\frac{8!}{(8-5)!\,5!} = \frac{8!}{3!\,5!} = 56$$

1, 8, 28, 56, 70, 56, 28...

The next two numbers are 8 and 1.

Note that there is a simple geometric way to generate this same sequence. It's called Pascal's triangle. Study the triangle illustrated on the following page. Each number on the inside of this triangle comes from adding the two numbers above it. If you happen to know about algebra, yet another way to make this triangle is to foil out $(x + y)^N$.

$$x + y$$

$$x^2 + 2xy + y^2$$

$$x^3 + 3x^2y + 3xy^2 + y^3$$

$$x^4 + 4x^3y + 6x^2y^2 + 4xy^3 + y^4$$

$$x^5 + 5x^4y + 10x^3y^2 + 10x^2y^3 + 5xy^4 + y^5$$

$$x^6 + 6x^5y + 15x^4y^2 + 20x^3y^3 + 15x^2y^4 + 6xy^5 + y^6$$

$$x^7 + 7x^6y + 21x^5y^2 + 35x^4y^3 + 35x^3y^4 + 21x^2y^5 + 7xy^6 + y^7$$

$$x^8 + 8x^7y + 28x^6y^2 + 56x^5y^3 + 70x^4y^4 + 56x^3y^5 + 28x^2y^6 + 8xy^7 + y^8$$

#1

1, 6, 120, 5040, 362880,

_____, _____

#2

1, 3, 15, 105, 945,

_____, _____, _____, _____

#3

1, 1, 2, 3, 8, 15, 48, 105, 384,

_____, _____, _____, _____

#4

2, 2, 4, 12, 48, 240,

_____, _____, _____, _____

#5

1, 1, 4, 36, 576, 14400,

_____, _____

#6

1, 7, 21, 35, 35, _____, _____, _____

#7

1, 9, 36, _____, _____, _____, _____, 36, 9, 1

#8

1, 4, 10, 20, 35, 56,

_____, _____, _____, _____

#9

2, 3, 8, 30, 144, 840, 5760,

_____, _____, _____, _____

#10

3628800, 1814400, 604800,

151200, 30240, 5040,

_____, _____, _____, _____

13 Negative Numbers

This chapter involves negative numbers. Recall that subtracting a negative number equates to addition. For example, $3 - (-2) = 3 + 2 = 5$. However, adding a negative number is like subtraction. For example, $7 + (-5) = 7 - 5 = 2$. Two more examples of adding or subtracting with negative numbers include $-6 + 3 = -3$ and $-1 - 4 = -5$.

When multiplying two numbers together, the answer is negative if the two numbers have opposite sign and positive if they have the same sign. For example, $3 \times (-4) = -12$, $-3 \times 4 = -12$, $3 \times 4 = 12$, and $-3 \times (-4) = 12$.

Example 1. This sequence repeatedly subtracts 2, starting with 6.

$$6, 4, 2, 0, -2, -4, -6...$$

The next two numbers are –8 (since –6 – 2 = –8) and –10 (since –8 – 2 = –10).

Example 2. In this sequence, each number is multiplied by –3.

$$1, -3, 9, -27, 81, -243...$$

The next two numbers are 729 (since –3 times –243 = 729) and –2187 (since –3 times 729 = –2187).

Example 3. This sequence is formed by taking the prime numbers and making every third number negative.

$$2, 3, -5, 7, 11, -13, 17...$$

The next two numbers are 19 and –23.

#1

$$-28, -24, -20, -16, -12,$$

$$-8, \underline{\quad}, \underline{\quad}, \underline{\quad}, \underline{\quad}$$

#2

$$-2, 4, -8, 16, -32, 64, \underline{\quad}, \underline{\quad}, \underline{\quad}, \underline{\quad}$$

#3

$$3, -5, 7, -7, 11, -9, 15,$$

$$-11, \underline{\quad}, \underline{\quad}, \underline{\quad}, \underline{\quad}$$

#4

$$-57, 43, -42, 35, -27, 27, -12,$$

$$19, \underline{\quad}, \underline{\quad}, \underline{\quad}, \underline{\quad}$$

#5

$$1, -3, -15, 45, 33, -99, -111, 333,$$

$$321, \underline{\quad}, \underline{\quad}, \underline{\quad}, \underline{\quad}$$

#6

$$0, 1, -1, 2, -3, 5, -8, 13,$$

$$-21, \underline{\quad}, \underline{\quad}, \underline{\quad}, \underline{\quad}$$

#7

-3, 4, -4, 3, -4, 4, -3, 4, -4,

3, -4, _____, _____, _____, _____

#8

20, 19, 17, 14, 10, 5, _____, _____, _____, _____

#9

3, 9, -9, 27, -27, -27, 81, -81, -81, -81,

243, -243, -243, _____, _____, _____, _____

#10

-6, -9, -15, -21, -33, -39, -51,

-57, -69, _____, _____, _____, _____

14 Fractions

The sequences of Chapter 14 involve fractions. Following is a brief refresher of some basic properties of fractions.

A fraction consists of a numerator and a denominator. For example, in $\frac{2}{5}$, the 2 is referred to as the numerator and the 5 is called the denominator.

When adding or subtracting fractions, first find a common denominator. The lowest common denominator can be found by examining the factors of each denominator.

For example, in $\frac{5}{6}$ and $\frac{7}{8}$, the lowest common denominator is 24. To see this, factor 6 as 2×3 and 8 as $2 \times 2 \times 2$. Both 6 and 8 share a common factor of 2. The lowest common denominator is $2 \times 2 \times 2 \times 3 = 24$, as both 6 and 8 can be made from this set of factors.

If you have trouble finding the lowest common denominator, an easier way to find a common denominator (but not necessarily the lowest) is to multiply the two denominators together. For example, with $\frac{5}{6}$ and $\frac{7}{8}$, if you multiply $6 \times 8 = 48$, you find that 48 is a possible common denominator (whereas the lowest common denominator in this case is 24).

Once you have a common denominator, multiply both the numerator and denominator of each fraction by the number needed to make that common denominator. For example, for $\frac{5}{6}$ and $\frac{7}{8}$, multiply $\frac{5}{6}$ by $\frac{4}{4}$ and $\frac{7}{8}$ by $\frac{3}{3}$ to make $\frac{20}{24}$ (since $5 \times 4 =$

20 and $6 \times 4 = 24$) and $\frac{21}{24}$ (since $7 \times 3 = 21$ and $8 \times 3 = 24$).

After you have a common denominator, you can add or subtract (as necessary) the numerators. For example,

$$\frac{5}{6} + \frac{7}{8} = \frac{20}{24} + \frac{21}{24} = \frac{41}{24}$$

(since $20 + 21 = 41$). Note that the common denominator remains unchanged.

Fractions can sometimes be reduced. This is the case when both the numerator and denominator share a common factor. It is considered good form to reduce fractions. For example, $\frac{42}{24}$ reduces to $\frac{7}{4}$, since both the numerator and denominator are divisible by 6 (that is, $42 \div 6 = 7$ and $24 \div 6 = 4$).

As another example, consider the fraction $\frac{18}{21}$. This can be reduced because both 18 and 21 are divisible by 3: $18 \div 3 = 6$ and $21 \div 3 = 7$. Therefore, $\frac{18}{21}$ reduces to $\frac{6}{7}$.

A fraction is said to be improper if the numerator exceeds the denominator. For example, $\frac{7}{4}$ is an improper fraction since 7 is greater than 4. This can alternatively be expressed as the mixed number $1\frac{3}{4}$. This is because $\frac{7}{4}$ can be written as $\frac{4}{4} + \frac{3}{4}$, and $\frac{4}{4}$ equals 1. So $\frac{7}{4}$ is 1 plus $\frac{3}{4}$, or $1\frac{3}{4}$.

When multiplying two fractions, simply multiply the numerators together and multiply the denominators together. For example, $\frac{2}{5} \times \frac{3}{4} = \frac{6}{20}$, which reduces to $\frac{3}{10}$. This is because $2 \times 3 = 6$ and $5 \times 4 = 20$, and because both 6 and 20 are divisible by 2 (since $6 \div 2 = 3$ and $20 \div 2 = 10$).

The reciprocal of a fraction is obtained by reversing the roles of the numerator and denominator. For example, the reciprocal of $\frac{3}{4}$ equals $\frac{4}{3}$. The reciprocal of an integer is simply 1 divided by the integer. For example, the reciprocal of 2 is $\frac{1}{2}$.

In order to divide two fractions, multiply the first number (the dividend) by the reciprocal of the second number (the divisor). For example, in $\frac{5}{6} \div \frac{2}{3}$, the first number $\left(\frac{5}{6}\right)$ is called the dividend and the second number $\left(\frac{2}{3}\right)$ is called the divisor. The reciprocal of $\frac{2}{3}$ is $\frac{3}{2}$. Therefore, $\frac{5}{6} \div \frac{2}{3}$ is equivalent to $\frac{5}{6} \times \frac{3}{2}$, which equals $\frac{15}{12}$ (since $5 \times 3 = 15$ and $6 \times 2 = 12$), which reduces to $\frac{5}{4}$ (since $15 \div 3 = 5$ and $12 \div 3 = 4$).

Example 1. In this sequence, the denominator grows by one.

$$1, \frac{1}{2}, \frac{1}{3}, \frac{1}{4}, \frac{1}{5}, \frac{1}{6}...$$

The next two numbers are $\frac{1}{7}$ and $\frac{1}{8}$.

Example 2. Here the numerators and denominators both grow by one. For example, $\frac{2}{5}$ becomes $\frac{3}{6}$ (since $2 + 1 = 3$ and $5 + 1 = 6$), but $\frac{3}{6}$ reduces to $\frac{1}{2}$. Next is $\frac{4}{7}$ (since $4 + 1 = 5$ and $6+1 = 7$), followed by $\frac{5}{8}$ and $\frac{6}{9}$. However, $\frac{6}{9}$ reduces to $\frac{2}{3}$.

$$\frac{2}{5}, \frac{1}{2}, \frac{4}{7}, \frac{5}{8}, \frac{2}{3}, \frac{7}{10}, \frac{8}{11}...$$

The next two numbers are $\frac{3}{4}$ (since $\frac{9}{12}$ reduces to $\frac{3}{4}$) and $\frac{10}{13}$.

Note that the sequence is really $\frac{2}{5}, \frac{3}{6}, \frac{4}{7}, \frac{5}{8}, \frac{6}{9}, \frac{7}{10}, \frac{8}{11}$, but $\frac{3}{6}$ reduces to $\frac{1}{2}$ and $\frac{6}{9}$ reduces to $\frac{2}{3}$.

Example 3. This sequence consists of $\frac{1}{16}, \frac{2}{16}$,

$\frac{3}{16}, \frac{4}{16}, \frac{5}{16}$, and so on, but expressed as decimals. For example, $\frac{1}{16}$ is 0.0625 and $\frac{2}{16}$ (equivalent to $\frac{1}{8}$) is 0.125.

$$0.0625, 0.125, 0.1875,$$
$$0.25, 0.3125, 0.375...$$

The next two numbers are 0.4375 and 0.5.

Example 4. This sequence adds $\frac{1}{3}$ to the previous number.

$$\frac{1}{3}, \frac{2}{3}, 1, 1\frac{1}{3}, 1\frac{2}{3}, 2, 2\frac{1}{3} ...$$

The next two numbers are $2\frac{2}{3}$ and 3.

#1

$$\frac{2}{3}, \frac{4}{5}, \frac{6}{7}, \frac{8}{9}, \frac{10}{11}, \underline{\quad}, \underline{\quad}, \underline{\quad}, \underline{\quad}$$

#2

$$\frac{1}{3}, \frac{5}{6}, \frac{1}{12}, \frac{23}{24}, \frac{1}{48}, \frac{95}{96}, \underline{\quad}, \underline{\quad}, \underline{\quad}, \underline{\quad}$$

#3

$$\frac{1}{4}, \frac{6}{7}, \frac{3}{8}, \frac{10}{11}, \frac{5}{12}, \frac{14}{15}, \frac{7}{16}, \frac{18}{19},$$ ____, ____, ____, ____

#4

$$\frac{1}{16}, \frac{1}{8}, \frac{3}{16}, \frac{1}{4}, \frac{5}{16}, \frac{3}{8}, \frac{7}{16},$$ ____, ____, ____, ____

#5

$$0.5, 0.25, 0.125, 0.0625,$$

$$0.03125, 0.015625, \underline{\hspace{3cm}},$$

$$\underline{\hspace{2.5cm}}, \underline{\hspace{2.5cm}}, \underline{\hspace{2.5cm}}$$

#6

$$\frac{1}{2}, 1\frac{1}{2}, 4\frac{1}{2}, 13\frac{1}{2}, 40\frac{1}{2}, 121\frac{1}{2},$$

$$\underline{\hspace{2cm}}, \underline{\hspace{2cm}}, \underline{\hspace{2cm}}, \underline{\hspace{2cm}}$$

#7

$$\frac{1}{5}, \frac{13}{15}, 1\frac{8}{15}, 2\frac{1}{5}, 2\frac{13}{15}, 3\frac{8}{15}, 4\frac{1}{5},$$

$$\underline{\hspace{2cm}}, \underline{\hspace{2cm}}, \underline{\hspace{2cm}}, \underline{\hspace{2cm}}$$

#8

$$\frac{1}{12}, \frac{1}{6}, \frac{1}{4}, \frac{1}{3}, \frac{5}{12}, \frac{1}{2},$$ ____, ____, ____, ____

#9

$$\frac{1}{2}, \frac{1}{3}, \frac{5}{6}, 1\frac{1}{6}, 2, 3\frac{1}{6}, 5\frac{1}{6}, 8\frac{1}{3}, 13\frac{1}{2},$$

———————, ———————, ———————, ———————

#10

$$4\frac{3}{7}, 5\frac{5}{9}, 6\frac{7}{11}, 9\frac{7}{13}, 8\frac{11}{15}, 13\frac{9}{17}, 10\frac{15}{19}, 17\frac{11}{21},$$

———————, ———————, ———————, ———————

#11

$$0.125, 0.5, 0.875, 1.25, 1.625,$$

———————, ———————, ———————, ———————

#12

$$\frac{2}{5}, \frac{3}{7}, \frac{5}{11}, \frac{7}{15}, \frac{11}{23}, \frac{13}{27}, \frac{17}{35},$$ ———, ———, ———, ———

#13

$$\frac{1}{2}, \frac{1}{3}, \frac{2}{9}, \frac{4}{27}, \frac{8}{81}, \frac{16}{243},$$ ———, ———, ———, ———

#14

$$\frac{1}{4}, \frac{9}{16}, \frac{25}{36}, \frac{49}{64}, \frac{81}{100},$$ ———, ———, ———, ———

#15

$$1, 2, 1\frac{1}{2}, 1\frac{1}{3}, 1, \frac{3}{4}, \frac{7}{13}, \frac{8}{21}, \frac{9}{34}, \underline{\quad}, \underline{\quad}, \underline{\quad}, \underline{\quad}$$

#16

$$\frac{1}{2}, \frac{1}{6}, \frac{5}{12}, \frac{1}{12}, \frac{1}{3}, 0, \frac{1}{4}, -\frac{1}{12}, \frac{1}{6}, -\frac{1}{6},$$

$$\frac{1}{12}, \underline{\quad}, \underline{\quad}, \underline{\quad}, \underline{\quad}$$

#17

$$0.\overline{5}, 1, 1.\overline{4}, 1.\overline{8}, 2.\overline{3}, 2.\overline{7}, 3.\overline{2}, 3.\overline{6},$$

$$\underline{\quad}, \underline{\quad}, \underline{\quad}, \underline{\quad}$$

#18

$$\frac{1}{3}, \frac{1}{2}, \frac{3}{4}, 1\frac{1}{8}, 1\frac{11}{16}, 2\frac{17}{32},$$

$$\underline{\quad}, \underline{\quad}, \underline{\quad}, \underline{\quad}$$

#19

$$\frac{1}{4}, 0.5, 75\%, 1, 1.25, 150\%, 1\frac{3}{4}, 2, 225\%,$$

$$\underline{\quad}, \underline{\quad}, \underline{\quad}, \underline{\quad}$$

#20

$$\frac{1}{2}, \frac{1}{3}, 1\frac{1}{2}, \frac{2}{9}, 6\frac{3}{4}, \frac{8}{243}, 205\frac{1}{32}, \underline{\quad}$$

15 Algebraic

Chapter 15 involves basic algebra. Following is a brief review of relevant basic algebra terminology and rules.

In the expression $3x + 2$, the symbol x is called the variable, while the numbers 3 and 2 are constants. The number 3 is called the coefficient of the variable x. The plus sign (+) separates two terms: One term is $3x$, the other is 2.

In the expression $3x^5$, the exponent 5 is called a power. Here, x is raised to the fifth power.

When two different powers of the same variable are multiplied together, add the powers. For example, $x^3 x^4 = x^7$ because $3 + 4 = 7$.

When two different powers of the same variable are divided, subtract the powers. For example, $\dfrac{x^8}{x^5} = x^3$ because $8 - 5 = 3$.

This is why $x^0 = 1$. For example, consider $\dfrac{x^3}{x^3} = 1$ (since any nonzero number divided by itself equals 1). According to the rule, $\dfrac{x^3}{x^3} = x^{3-3} = x^0$. The last two equations can only both be true if $x^0 = 1$.

When distributing across parentheses, multiply every term in parentheses by the outside expression. For example,

$$3x(x^2 - 2) = 3x^3 - 6x$$

since $3x(x^2) = 3x^3$ and $3x(-2) = -6x$. As another example, $-2(x - 4) = -2x + 8$ since $-2(x) = -2x$ and $-2(-4) = 8$.

The opposite of distributing is factoring. For example, $6x^4 + 9x^2$ can be factored by pulling out the common term of $3x^2$.

The result equals $3x^2(2x^2 + 3)$, since $3x^2(2x^2) = 6x^4$ and $3x^2(3) = 9x^2$.

Example 1. This sequence consists of powers of x, beginning with x^0, which equals one. Next is x^1, which equals x, followed by x^2, x^3, x^4, and so on.

$$1, x, x^2, x^3, x^4, x^5...$$

The next two elements are x^6 and x^7.

Example 2. This pattern grows one term at a time, beginning with x^{12}, where each new terms adds 1 to the coefficient and reduces the power by 1. Add $2x^{11}$ to get $x^{12} + 2x^{11}$. Then add $3x^{10}$ to get $x^{12} + 2x^{11} + 3x^{10}$. The next term to add is $4x^9$, which gives $x^{12} + 2x^{11} + 3x^{10} + 4x^9$.

$$x^{12}, x^{12} + 2x^{11}, x^{12} + 2x^{11} + 3x^{10},$$
$$x^{12} + 2x^{11} + 3x^{10} + 4x^9,$$
$$x^{12} + 2x^{11} + 3x^{10} + 4x^9 + 5x^8...$$

The next two elements are $x^{12} + 2x^{11} + 3x^{10} + 4x^9 + 5x^8 + 6x^7$ and $x^{12} + 2x^{11} + 3x^{10} + 4x^9 + 5x^8 + 6x^7 + 7x^6$.

Example 3. This sequence begins with $2x$ and $3x$, and multiplies the previous two terms together. The next element is $6x^2$. Now multiply $3x$ by $6x^2$ to make $18x^3$. Next, $6x^2$ times $18x^3$ makes $108x^5$.

$$2x, 3x, 6x^2, 18x^3, 108x^5...$$

The next two elements are $1944x^8$ (since $18 \times 108 = 1944$ and $x^3x^5 = x^8$) and $209952x^{13}$ (since $108 \times 1944 = 209952$ and $x^5x^8 = x^{13}$).

#1
$$x^{10}, 10x^9, 90x^8, 720x^7,$$

_____, _____, _____, _____

#2
$$120, 120x, 60x^2, 20x^3, 5x^4,$$

_____, _____, _____, _____

#3
$$4x, 9x^2, 16x^4, 25x^8, 36x^{16},$$

_____ , _____ , _____ , _____

#4
$$2, 3x^2, 5x^4, 7x^6, 11x^8, 13x^{10}, 17x^{12},$$

_____ , _____ , _____ , _____

#5
$$x, \frac{2}{x^2}, \frac{x^3}{6}, \frac{24}{x^5}, \frac{x^8}{120}, \frac{720}{x^{13}}, \underline{\quad}, \underline{\quad}, \underline{\quad}, \underline{\quad}$$

#6
$$2x^4, 7x^{11}, 16x^{22}, 29x^{37}, 46x^{56},$$

_____ , _____ , _____ , _____

#7
$$(a + 2)^3, (b + 4)^6, (c + 8)^{12}, (d + 16)^{24},$$

_____ , _____ , _____ , _____

#8
$$\frac{x^4}{24}, \frac{x^3}{12}, \frac{x^2}{4}, x, \underline{\quad}, \underline{\quad}, \underline{\quad}, \underline{\quad}, \frac{15120}{x^4}$$

#9

$2^a, c^4, 8^e, g^{16}, 32^i,$ ____, ____, ____, ____

#10

$7, 2^3, 3^2, 2{\cdot}5, 11, 2^2{\cdot}3, 13, 2{\cdot}7, 3{\cdot}5, 2^4,$

_____, _____, _____, _____

#11

$5x^2, 7x^3, 11x^5, 19x^9, 35x^{17}, 67x^{33},$

_____, _____, _____, _____

#12

$3x^2, x^5, 4x^3, 2x^6, 5x^4, 3x^7, 6x^5,$

_____, _____, _____, _____

#13

$x, 2x^{\frac{1}{2}}, \dfrac{x^2}{2}, \dfrac{2x^{\frac{3}{2}}}{3}, \dfrac{x^5}{5}, \dfrac{2x^{\frac{5}{2}}}{5}, \dfrac{x^{10}}{10}, \dfrac{2x^{\frac{7}{2}}}{7}, \dfrac{x^{17}}{17}, \dfrac{2x^{\frac{9}{2}}}{9},$

$\dfrac{x^{26}}{26}, \dfrac{2x^{\frac{11}{2}}}{11}, \dfrac{x^{37}}{37},$ ____, ____, ____, ____

#14

$$\frac{8x^{\frac{1}{8}}}{3}, 2x^{\frac{1}{4}}, \frac{8x^{\frac{3}{8}}}{5}, \frac{4x^{\frac{1}{2}}}{3}, \frac{8x^{\frac{5}{8}}}{7}, x^{\frac{3}{4}}, \frac{8x^{\frac{7}{8}}}{9},$$

_____, _____, _____, _____

#15

$$2x + 1, x - 3, 3x - 2, 4x - 5, 7x - 7,$$
$$11x - 12, 18x - 19, 29x - 31,$$

_____, _____, _____, _____

#16

$$x, y, x^2, xy, y^2, x^3, x^2y, xy^2, y^3,$$

_____, _____, _____, _____

#17

$$2x^5, 7x^3, 5x^{11}, 15x^7, 11x^{23}, 27x^{13}, 17x^{35},$$

_____, _____, _____, _____

#18

$$3x + 4 = x^2,$$

$$3x = x^2 - 4,$$

$$6x = 2x^2 - 8,$$

$$6x - 4 = 2x^2 - 12,$$

$$12x - 8 = 4x^2 - 24,$$

$$12x - 12 = 4x^2 - 28,$$

$$24x - 24 = 8x^2 - 56,$$

$$24x - 28 = 8x^2 - 60,$$

_____,

_____,

_____,

_____

#19

$$x^3,$$

$$x^4 + 3x^3,$$

$$x^5 + 4x^4 + 5x^3,$$

$$x^6 + 5x^5 + 6x^4 + 11x^3,$$

$$x^7 + 6x^6 + 7x^5 + 13x^4 + 20x^3,$$

$$x^8 + 7x^7 + 8x^6 + 15x^5 + 23x^4 + 38x^3,$$

_____,

_____

#20

1,

$$x + y,$$

$$x^2 + 2xy + y^2,$$

$$x^3 + 3x^2y + 3xy^2 + y^3,$$

$$x^4 + 4x^3y + 6x^2y^2 + 4xy^3 + y^4,$$

$$x^5 + 5x^4y + 10x^3y^2 + 10x^2y^3 + 5xy^4 + y^5,$$

$$x^6 + 6x^5y + 15x^4y^2 + 20x^3y^3 + 15x^2y^4 + 6xy^5 + y^6,$$

—————————————————————,

———————————————————

16 Visual

The patterns in this chapter involve pictures. Solving these puzzles involves visual pattern recognition.

Example 1. The black square moves one space clockwise along the large square.

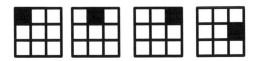

Example 2. This shape rotates 45° clockwise.

Example 3. Add the top and left numbers to make the right number.

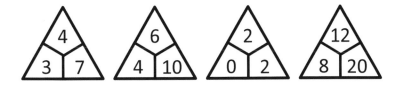

#1 Shade the correct triangles in the last figure.

#2 Draw the shape that comes next.

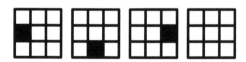

#3 Draw the shape that comes next.

#4 Shade the correct square in the last figure.

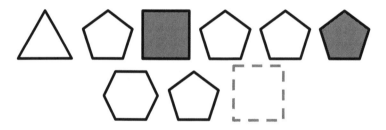

#5 Fill in the missing number.

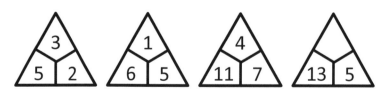

#6 Draw the shape that comes next.

#7 Draw the shape that comes next.

#8 Fill in the missing number.

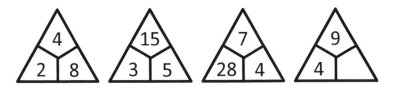

#9 Shade the correct square in the last figure.

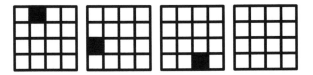

#10 Draw the shape that comes next.

#11 Draw the shape that comes next.

#12 Draw the shape that comes next.

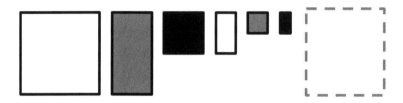

#13 Draw the shape that comes next.

#14 Color the correct squares in the last figure.

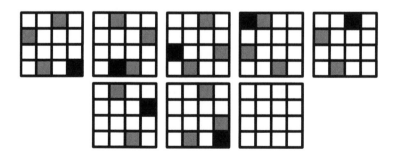

#15 Shade the correct squares in the last figure.

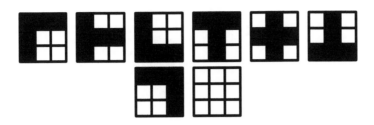

#16 Fill in the missing number.

3	4		2	8		1	9		5	6		7	9
5	7		7	9		3	6		10	20		13	

#17 Color the correct squares in the last figure.

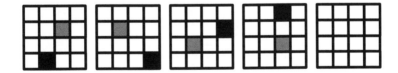

#18 Draw the shape that comes next.

#19 Draw the shape that comes next.

#20 Color the correct squares in the last figure.

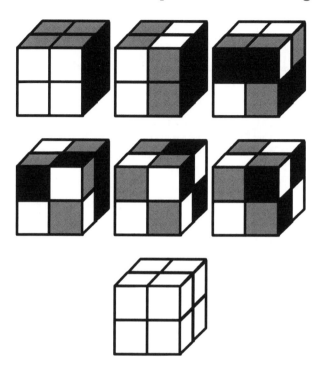

17 Arrays

In this chapter, the patterns come in the form of arrays. Each array has rows and columns. Some of the arrays are numerical, while others have visual elements.

Example 1. In the array that follows, odd numbers are arranged in order from left to right, top to bottom.

3	5	7
9	11	13
15	17	19

Example 2. In the following array, the top row is in order (2, 3, and 4), the middle row doubles the top row ($2 \times 2 = 4$, $3 \times 2 = 6$, and $4 \times 2 = 8$), and the bottom row squares the top row ($2^2 = 4$, $3^2 = 9$, and $4^2 = 16$).

2	3	4
4	6	8
4	9	16

Example 3. The pattern ♥, ♥, and ✦ is used to make the following array.

♥	♥	✦	♥
♥	✦	♥	♥
✦	♥	♥	✦
♥	♥	✦	♥

Instructions: Fill in the missing elements.

#1#

8	16	24
32	40	
56		72

#2#

95	84	73
62		40
29	18	

#3#

3	6	12
4	8	
5		20

#4#

2	7	17
3		19
5	13	

#5#

4	3	8
9	5	1
	7	

#6#

4	6	9	11
16	18	25	27
36	38	49	
64			

#7#

●	●	◆	●
◆	●	●	◆
●	◆	●	
◆			

#8#

14	17		20
10	13	16	18
7	9	12	
5	6		

#9#

1	1	0	
2		7	14
3	27	26	52
	64		126

#10#

II	IV	VIII
XVI	XXXII	
CXXVIII		DXII

#11#

1	2	5	6
4	3	8	7
9	10		
12	11		

#12#

2	3	5	9
2049		8193	17
	32769	16385	33
513		129	

#13#

5	8	■	14
17	■	23	26
■	32		■
	44	■	

#14#

1	2	3	4
2	3	5	7
3	5	8	
4	8		20

#15#

2	1	1
8	5	3
	21	

18 Analogies

These puzzles involve analogies. They are solved with logical inference. In particular, they involve finding the similarities between relationships and using that to predict further similarity between them.

In this book, analogies will be expressed with the following notation:

AA : aa :: BB : bb

This reads as, "**AA** is to **aa** as **BB** is to **bb**." The first colon (:) equates to the phrase "is to." The pair of colons (::) in the middle equates to the word "as." The last colon (:) equates to the phrase "is to."

AA and **aa** are related to one another. **BB** and **bb** are related to one another in a similar way. The two relationships are analogous to one another; i.e. they form an analogy.

The concept of the analogy as well as the notation are illustrated with the following examples.

Example 1. finger : hand :: toe : ___

A finger is to a hand as a toe is to a foot. A hand has 5 fingers and a foot has 5 toes. Therefore, the word "foot" completes this analogy.

Example 2. 5 : 25 :: 7 : ___

5 is to 25 as 7 is to 49. The expression 5 : 25 is related to 7 : 49 by squaring: $5^2 = 25$ and $7^2 = 49$.

Example 3. → : ↔ :: ↑ : ___

→ is to ↔ as ↑ is to ↕. The horizontal arrow turns into a horizontal double arrow. Therefore, the vertical arrow turns into a vertical double arrow.

Instructions: Select the answer to each multiple choice question that best completes the analogy.

#1

three : 27 :: four : _____

(A) 8   (B) 12   (C) 16   (D) 64

#2

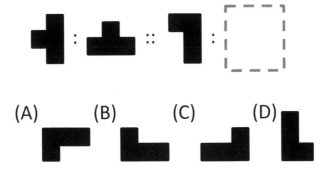

#3

hand : wrist :: foot : _____

(A) ankle   (B) leg   (C) sole   (D) toe

#4

$$81 : 9 :: 36 : \underline{\qquad}$$

(A) 2　(B) 3　(C) 6　(D) 12

#5

century : year :: meter : _____

(A) centimeter　(B) inch

(C) millimeter　(D) yard

#6

ADE : 145 :: CFH : _____

(A) 2　(B) 367　(C) 368　(D) 389

#7

#8

moon : earth :: Venus : _____

(A) Mercury (B) Mars

(C) sun (D) Uranus

#9

circle : circumference :: square : _____

(A) area (B) diameter

(C) diagonal (D) perimeter

#10

$(3, 4, 5) : 35 :: (6, 7, 8) :$ _____

(A) 42 (B) 48 (C) 86 (D) 104

#11

uncle : nephew :: aunt : _____

(A) cousin (B) daughter

(C) mother (D) niece

#12

$(10, 11) : 101 :: (100, 101) :$ _____

(A) 110   (B) 111   (C) 1001   (D) 1101

#13

horse : foal :: deer : _____

(A) calf   (B) colt   (C) fawn   (D) filly

#14

rectangle : square :: parallelogram : _____

(A) octahedron   (B) quadrilateral

(C) rhombus   (D) trapezoid

#15

$$\frac{5}{8} : 1\frac{1}{4} :: \frac{3}{4} : \text{\_\_\_\_}$$

(A) $1\frac{1}{4}$ (B) $1\frac{1}{2}$ (C) $2\frac{1}{4}$ (D) $2\frac{1}{2}$

#16

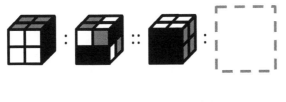

#17

$$\left(8, \frac{2}{3}\right) : 4 :: \left(81, \frac{3}{4}\right) : \_\_\_$$

(A) 6   (B) 9   (C) 18   (D) 27

#18

COCCOON : C_3O_3N : : COCOA : _____

(A) A_3C_3O (B) C_2O_2A

(C) C_2OA_2 (D) $C_6H_{12}O_6$

#19

circle : sphere : : square : _____

(A) cube   (B) cylinder

(C) diamond   (D) rectangle

#20

PUZZLES : OTYYKDR :: PATTERNS : _____

(A) OZSSDQMR   (B) OBYYGXFJ

(C) QZXXHPJK   (D) QBUUFSO

Answers

1 Ordered

(1) 7, **9**, 11, **13**, **15**, 17, 19, **21**
Count odd numbers, starting with 7.

(2) 5, **10**, 15, **20**, **25**, 30, **35**, 40
Count by 5.

(3) **500**, 600, 700, **800**, 900, **1000**, **1100**, 1200
Count by 100.

(4) 25, 50, **75**, **100**, 125, **150**, 175, **200**
Count by 25.

(5) **53**, 65, 77, **89**, **101**, 113, **125**, 137
Count by 12.

(6) b, d, f, **h**, j, **l**, **n**, p
Skip every other letter (b, not c, d, not e, f, not g, h, not i, etc.).

(7) c, g, k, **o**, s, **w**
Skip three letters (c, skip d-e-f, g, skip h-i-j, k, skip l-m-n, etc.).

(8)
Draw polygons which have an even number of sides.

(9)
Add one star point.

(10) 15, **14**, 13, **12**, 11, **10**, **9**, 8

Count backwards.

(11) **30**, 27, 24, 21, **18**, 15, **12**, **9**

Subtract 3.

(12) 125, **120**, 115, **110**, **105**, 100, **95**, 90

Subtract 5.

(13) **1100**, 1075, 1050, **1025**, **1000**, **975**, 950, 925

Subtract 25.

(14) **x**, w, v, **u**, t, s, r, **q**

Write the alphabet backwards, starting with x.

(15) q, **o**, m, **k**, i, **g**, e, c

Skip every other letter, going backwards.

(16) y, v, **s**, p, **m**, **j**, g, d

Skip two letters, going backwards (y, skip x-w, v, skip u-t, s, skip r-q, etc.).

(17)

Draw a polygon with one less side.

(18)

Draw one less star point.

(19) A, **E**, I, O, U

Write the vowels in order.

(20) d, f, g, h, **j**, **k**, l, m, n, **p**, q

Write the consonants in order, beginning with d (thus e, i, and o are skipped).

2 Patterned

(1) 0, 1, 0, 1, 0, **1**, **0**, **1**

Alternate 0 and 1.

(2) t, **y**, **t**, **y**, t, y, t, y

Alternate t and y.

(3) A, a, **A**, a, A, a, A, a, **A**, **a**

Alternate A and a.

(4) 2, 4, 8, 2, 4, 8, 2, **4**, **8**, **2**

Repeat 2, 4, and 8.

(5) z, x, q, z, x, q, z, x, **q**, **z**, **x**

Repeat z, x, and q.

(6)

Repeat heart, star, and moon.

(7) 9, 9, 4, 9, 9, 4, 9, **9**, **4**, **9**

Repeat 9, 9, and 4.

(8) 3, 5, 3, 3, 5, 3, 3, **5**, **3**, **3**

Repeat 3, 5, and 3.

(9) G, g, g, G, g, g, **G**, **g**, **g**, G

Repeat G, g, and g.

(10) F, F, e, F, **F**, e, F, F, **e**, **F**

Repeat F, F, and e.

(11) ☺, ☹, ☺, ☺, ☹, ☺, ☺, ☹, ☺, ☺

Repeat smile, frown, and smile.

(12) 2, 5, 3, 9, 2, 5, 3, 9, 2, 5, **3**, **9**, **2**

Repeat 2, 5, 3, and 9.

(13) 1, 7, 6, 4, 8, 1, 7, 6, 4, 8, 1, 7, 6, **4, 8, 1**
Repeat 1, 7, 6, 4, and 8.

(14) D, b, P, q, D, b, P, q, D, b, P, **q, D, b**
Repeat D, b, P, and q.

(15) C, e, H, j, c, E, h, J, C, e, H, **j, c, E**
Repeat C, e, H, j, c, E, h, and J.

(16) 8, 2, 8, 8, 2, 8, 8, 8, 2, 8, 8, 8, 8, 2, 8, 8, 8, **8, 8, 2**
Steadily increase the number of 8's between the 2's (one 8, 2, two 8's, 2, three 8's, 2, etc.).

(17) 6, **77**, 888, **9999**, 1010101010, 111111111111, 12121212121212, **1313131313131313**
Write one 6, two 7's, three 8's, four 9's, five 10's, etc.

(18) 2, 23, 234, 2345, **23456, 234567, 2345678**
Add one more digit to the list, in order.

(19) 1, 31, **531**, 7531, 97531, 1197531, **131197531**, **15131197531**
Insert the next odd number on the left (insert 11 to the left of 97531 to get 1197531, for example, then insert 13 to the left of this to get 131197531).

(20) 4, 4, 3, 12, 12, 9, 36, 36, 27, **108, 108, 81, 324**
Triple 4, 4, and 3 to get 12, 12, and 9 (4 × 3 = 12 and 3 × 3 = 9). Triple 12, 12, and 9 to get 36, 36, and 27 (12 × 3 = 36 and 9 × 3 = 27). Repeat this pattern.

3 Alternating

(1) 11, 99, 22, 88, **33, 77**, 44, 66, **55, 55**, 66, 44
The sequence 11, 22, 33, etc. is mixed with 99, 88, 77, etc.

(2) 3, 18, 6, 16, 9, 14, 12, 12, **15, 10, 18, 8**
The sequence 3, 6, 9, etc. adds 3, while the sequence 18, 16, 14, etc. subtracts 2.

(3) 6, 24, 12, **24**, **18**, 24, 24, 24, 30, **24**, **36**

The sequence 6, 12, 18, etc. adds 6, while the sequence 24, 24, 24, etc. repeats the same number over and over.

(4) 5, 6, 7, 9, 9, 12, 11, 15, **13**, **18**, **15**, **21**

The sequence 5, 7, 9, etc. consists of odd numbers, while the sequence 6, 9, 12, etc. adds 3.

(5) 10, 50, 15, 40, 20, 30, 25, **20**, **30**, **10**, **35**

The sequence 10, 15, 20, etc. adds 5, while the sequence 50, 40, 30, etc. subtracts 10.

(6) p, q, o, r, n, s, m, **t**, **l**, **u**, **k**

The sequence p, o, n, etc. is the reverse alphabet, while the sequence q, r, s, etc. is forward.

(7) **Z**, **N**, **X**, **O**, V, P, T, Q, R, R, P

The sequence Z, X, V, T, etc. skips every other letter going backwards, while the sequence N, O, P, etc. goes forward without skipping.

(8) c, f, d, **f**, **e**, f, f, f, g, f, h, **f**, **i**

The sequence c, d, e, etc. is the alphabet beginning with c, while the sequence f, f, f, etc. repeats f over and over.

(9) J, 29, L, 26, N, 23, P, 20, **R**, **17**, **T**, **14**

The sequence J, L, N, etc. skips every other letter, while the sequence 29, 26, 23, etc. subtracts 3.

(10) 7, z, **11**, **w**, 15, t, 19, **q**, **23**, n

The sequence 7, 11, 15, etc. adds 4, while the sequence z, w, t, etc. skips two letters going backward (z, skip y-x, w, skip v-u, t, skip s-r, q, etc.).

(11)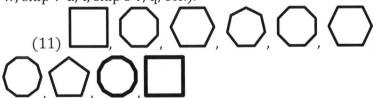

The sequence square, hexagon, octagon, etc. adds 2 sides, while the sequence octagon, heptagon, hexagon, etc. subtracts 1 side.

(12)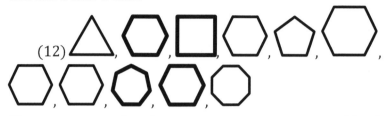

The sequence triangle, square, pentagon, etc. adds 1 side, while the sequence hexagon, hexagon, hexagon, etc. repeats the same shape over and over.

(13)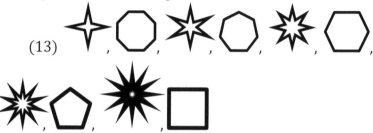

The sequence star 4, star 6, star 8, etc. adds 2 star points, while the sequence octagon, heptagon, hexagon, etc. subtracts 1 side.

(14) →, ↑, ↓, ↓, ←, ↑, ↑, ↓, →, ↑, ↓, ↓, ←, ↑

The sequence right (→), down (↓), left (←), up (↑), etc. rotates 90° clockwise, while the sequence up (↑), down (↓), up (↑), down (↓), etc. flips repeatedly.

(15) ↑, ←, ←, ↖, ↓, ↑, →, ↗, ↑, →, ←, ↘, ↓, ↓

The sequence 90° (↑), 180° (←), 270° (↓), etc. rotates 90° counterclockwise, while the sequence 180° (←), 135° (↖), 90° (↑), etc. rotates 45° clockwise.

(16) Q, z, X, w, **Q**, z, **X**, w, **Q**, **z**, X, w, Q

This is just Q, z, X, w repeating itself.

(17) 1, 0, 0, 0, 1, 1, 0, 0, 1, 0, 0, 1, 1, 0, 0, 0, 1, 1, 0, 0, **1, 0, 0, 1**

The sequence 1, 0, 1, 0, 1, etc. simply alternates 1's and 0's, and this sequence is merged together with the sequence 0, 0, 1, 0, 0, 1 etc. (which repeats 0, 0, and 1).

(18) D, e, f, F, H, g, j, H, L, i, n, **J, P, k, r**

The sequence D, f, H, j, L, etc. skips every other letter and alternates case, while the sequence e, F, g, H, I, etc. is the alphabet changing case.

(19) 30, 70, 25, 35, 60, 35, 40, 50, 45, 45, 40, 55, 50, 30, 65, 55, **20, 75, 60, 10**

Three patterns are merged together: The sequence 30, 35, 40, etc. adds 5, the sequence 70, 60, 50, etc. subtracts 10, and the sequence 25, 35, 45, etc. adds 10.

(20) K, h, Q, L, i, P, M, j, O, N, k, N, O, l, M, P, **m, L, Q, n**

Three patterns are merged together: The sequence K, L, M, etc. is the uppercase alphabet, the sequence h, i, j, etc. is the lowercase alphabet, and the sequence Q, P, O, etc. is the uppercase alphabet backwards.

4 Cyclic

(1) 927, 279, 792, 927, 279, **792, 927, 279, 792**

These digits cycle in the order 927, 279, and 792 repeatedly.

(2) 3841, 8413, 4138, 1384, 3841, **8413, 4138, 1384, 3841**

These digits cycle in the order 3841, 8413, 4138, and 1384 repeatedly. (Move the first digit to the end each time. For example, 3841 turns into 8413.)

(3) 4, 6, 8, 0, 2, 4, 6, **8, 0, 2, 4**

These single-digit even numbers cycle in order.

(4) **7**, **88**, **999**, **0000**, 11111, 222222, **3333333**, **44444444**
The digits 7, 8, 9, 0, 1, 2, etc. cycle in order, increasing the number of digits by one each time.

(5) 123, 132, 231, **213**, **312**, 321, 123, 132, **231**, **213**
The digits 1, 2, and 3 cycle through all possible 3-digit permutations: 123, 132, 231, 213, 312, and 321. (Every other one, 123, 231, and 312 has the digits 1, 2, 3, 1, and 2 in order.)

(6) act, cta, tac, act, cta, **tac**, **act**, **cta**, **tac**
These letters cycle in the order act, cta, and tac repeatedly.

(7) spot, **pots**, **otsp**, tspo, spot, pots, **otsp**, **tspo**
These letters cycle in the order spot, pots, otsp, and tspo repeatedly. (Move the first letter to the end each time. For example, spot turns into pots.)

(8) u, w, **y**, **a**, c, **e**, g, **i**, k
The alphabet is cyclic, if after z comes a. This pattern skips every other letter: u, skip v, w, skip x, y, skip z, a, skip b, c, etc.

(9) ccccccccc, bbbbbbbb, **aaaaaaa**, **zzzzzz**, yyyyy, **xxxx**, www, **vv**
The alphabet appears in reverse, with z following a, removing one letter each time.

(10) Roygbiv, rOygbiv, **roYgbiv**, royGbiv, **roygBiv**, **roygblv**, roygbiV, Roygbiv, **rOygbiv**
The letters roygbiv are repeated, with one uppercase letter. The placement of the uppercase letter advances each time, returning to the beginning after reaching the end. (Note that roygbiv is an acronym for red, orange, yellow, green, blue, indigo, and violet, which are the

colors of the primary rainbow from top to bottom. However, it's not necessary to know this acronym to solve the puzzle.)

(11) 0, 11, **222**, 3333, 222, **11**, 0, 11, **222**, 3333, **222**
This sequence increases from 0, 11, 222, to 333, then decreases 222, 11, to 0, and continues to increase and decrease this way.

(12) CIRCLE, IRCLEC, **RCLECI**, CLECIR, **LECIRC**, ECIRCL, **CIRCLE**, IRCLEC, **RCLECI**
The first letter of one word becomes the last letter of the next word. For example, move the I of IRCLEC to the end, forming RCLECI.

(13) 10:45, 11:15, **11:45**, **12:15**, 12:45, **1:15**, **1:45**, 2:15
Add 30 minutes.

(14) 9:30, **10:15**, 11:00, 11:45, **12:30**, **1:15**, 2:00, **2:45**
Add 45 minutes.

(15) Friday, **Saturday**, **Sunday**, Monday, **Tuesday**, Wednesday, **Thursday**, Friday
The days of the week appear in order.

(16) October, November, **December**, **January**, February, **March**, April, **May**
The months appear in order.

(17) north, **east**, south, west, north, **east**, **south**, **west**
The compass directions cycle in the order north, east, south, and west.

(18) east, northeast, north, **northwest**, west, southwest, **south**, southeast, **east**, **northeast**
Rotate 45° counterclockwise.

(19) north, southeast, west, northeast, south, northwest, **east**, **southwest**, **north**, **southeast**

Rotate 135° clockwise.

(20) 90° (↑), 180° (←), 270° (↓), 360° (→), 90° (↑), **180° (←), 270° (↓), 360° (→), 90° (↑)**

Rotate 90° counterclockwise.

5 Additive & Multiplicative

(1) 6, 12, 18, 24, **30**, **36**, **42**, **48**

Add 6.

(2) 72, 64, 56, 48, **40**, **32**, **24**, **16**

Subtract 8.

(3) **1**, **2**, 4, 8, 16, 32, **64**, **128**

Double each number.

(4) 7, 13, **19**, **25**, 31, 37, **43**, **49**

Add 6.

(5) 640, 320, 160, 80, **40**, **20**, **10**, **5**

Cut in half.

(6) **33**, 37, 41, **45**, **49**, 53, 57, **61**

Add 4.

(7) **52**, **45**, 38, 31, **24**, 17, 10, **3**

Subtract 7.

(8) 25, **50**, **100**, **200**, **400**, 800, 1600, 3200

Double each number.

(9) 6, **11**, 16, **21**, 26, **31**, 36, **41**

Add 5.

(10) **1**, 20, **39**, 58, **77**, 96, **115**, 134

Add 19.

(11) 9, 18, **27**, **36**, 45, **54**, 63, **72**

Add 9.

(12) **46**, 40, 34, 28, **22**, **16**, 10, **4**

Subtract 6.

(13) 8, 16, **32**, 64, **128**, **256**, 512, **1024**

Double each number.

(14) **9**, 21, 33, **45**, 57, 69, **81**, **93**

Add 12.

(15) 768, 384, 192, 96, **48**, **24**, **12**, **6**

Cut in half.

(16) 212, **199**, 186, 173, **160**, 147, **134**, **121**

Subtract 13.

(17) **2**, **6**, 18, **54**, 162, 486, 1458, **4374**

Multiply by 3.

(18) 192, **216**, **240**, 264, 288, 312, **336**, **360**

Add 24.

(19) **2**, **10**, 50, 250, 1250, 6250, **31250**, **156250**

Multiply by 5.

(20) 2187, 729, 243, 81, **27**, **9**, **3**, **1**

Divide by 3.

6 Multiple Operations

(1) 2, 7, 22, 67, 202, **607**, **1822**, **5467**, **16402**

Multiply by 3 and add 1. For example, $3 \times 2 + 1 = 6 + 1 = 7$ and $3 \times 7 + 1 = 21 + 1 = 22$.

(2) 3, 9, 8, 14, 13, 19, 18, **24**, **23**, **29**, **28**

Add 6, subtract 1, add 6, subtract 1, repeating this pattern. For example, $3 + 6 = 9$, $9 - 1 = 8$, $8 + 6 = 14$, and $14 - 1 = 13$.

(3) 1022, 510, 254, 126, 62, **30**, **14**, **6**, **2**

Divide by 2 and subtract 1. For example, $1022 \div 2 - 1 = 511 - 1 = 510$ and $510 \div 2 - 1 = 255 - 1 = 254$.

(4) 1, 3, 6, 18, 36, 108, 216, **648**, **1296**, **3888**, **7776**

Triple, double, triple, double, repeating this pattern. For

example, $1 \times 3 = 3$, $3 \times 2 = 6$, $6 \times 3 = 18$, and $18 \times 2 = 36$.

(5) 101, 99, 95, 93, 89, **87, 83, 81, 77**

Subtract 2, subtract 4, subtract 2, subtract 4, repeating this pattern. For example, $101 - 2 = 99$, $99 - 4 = 95$, $95 - 2 = 93$, and $93 - 4 = 89$.

(6) 256, 128, 144, 72, 88, 44, 60, **30, 46, 23, 39**

Divide by 2, add 16, divide by 2, add 16, repeating this pattern. For example, $256 \div 2 = 128$, $128 + 16 = 144$, $144 \div 2 = 72$, and $72 + 16 = 88$.

(7) 3, 5, 9, **17**, 33, **65, 129**, 257, **513**

Multiply by 2 and subtract 1. For example, $3 \times 2 - 1 = 6 - 1 = 5$ and $5 \times 2 - 1 = 10 - 1 = 9$.

(8) 5, 7, 15, 17, 35, 37, 75, 77, 155, **157, 315, 317, 635**

Add 2, next double and add 1, add 2, next double and add 1, repeating this pattern. For example, $5 + 2 = 7$, $7 \times 2 + 1 = 15$, $15 + 2 = 17$, $17 \times 2 + 1 = 35$, $35 + 2 = 37$, and $37 \times 2 + 1 = 75$.

(9) 1, 3, 6, 10, 15, 21, **28, 36, 45, 55**

Add 2, add 3, add 4, add 5, add 6, etc., always adding one more. For example, $1 + 2 = 3$, $3 + 3 = 6$, $6 + 4 = 10$, and $10 + 5 = 15$.

(10) 4, 6, 9, 13, 18, 24, **31, 39, 48, 58**

Add 2, add 3, add 4, add 5, add 6, etc., always adding one more. For example, $4 + 2 = 6$, $6 + 3 = 9$, $9 + 4 = 13$, $13 + 5 = 18$, etc.

(11) 100, 51, 98, 53, 95, 56, 91, 60, **86, 65, 80, 71**

This alternating sequence has two patterns merged together. One subtracts 2, subtracts 3, subtracts 4, etc. (100, 98, 95, 91, etc.), while the other adds 2, adds 3, adds 4, etc. (51, 53, 56, 60, etc.).

(12) 8, 4, 12, 6, 24, 12, 60, 30, 180, 90, 630, **315, 2520, 1260, 11340**

Cut in half, multiply by 3, cut in half, multiply by 4, cut in half, multiply by 5, etc. For example, $8 \div 2 = 4$, $4 \times 3 = 12$, $12 \div 2 = 6$, $6 \times 4 = 24$, $24 \div 2 = 12$, $12 \times 5 = 60$, $60 \div 2 = 30$, and $30 \times 6 = 180$.

(13) 50, 52, 47, 55, 43, 59, 38, 64, 32, **70, 25, 77, 17**

This alternating sequence has two patterns merged together. One subtracts 3, subtracts 4, subtracts 5, etc. (50, 47, 43, 38, etc.), while the other adds 3, adds 4, adds 5, etc. (52, 55, 59, 64, etc.).

(14) 10, 50, 20, 100, 70, 350, 320, 1600, **1570, 7850, 7820, 39100**

Multiply by 5, subtract 30, multiply by 5, subtract 30, repeating this pattern. For example, $10 \times 5 = 50$, $50 - 30 = 20$, $20 \times 5 = 100$, and $100 - 30 = 70$.

(15) 1, 3, 6, 9, 18, 22, 44, 49, 98, **104, 208, 215, 430**

Add 2, double, add 3, double, add 4, double, add 5, double, add 6, repeating this pattern. For example, $1 + 2 = 3$, $3 \times 2 = 6$, $6 + 3 = 9$, $9 \times 2 = 18$, $18 + 4 = 22$, $22 \times 2 = 44$, $44 + 5 = 49$, and $49 \times 2 = 98$.

(16) 2, 2, 1, 2, 1, 3, 2, 8, 7, 35, 34, **204, 203, 1421, 1420**

Multiply by 1, subtract 1, multiply by 2, subtract 1, multiply by 3, subtract 1, multiply by 4, subtract 1, multiply by 5, subtract 1, repeating this pattern. For example, $2 \times 1 = 2$, $2 - 1 = 1$, $1 \times 2 = 2$, $2 - 1 = 1$, $1 \times 3 = 3$, $3 - 1 = 2$, $2 \times 4 = 8$, $8 - 1 = 7$, $7 \times 5 = 35$, and $35 - 1 = 34$.

(17) a, d, c, f, e, h, g, j, i, l, k, **n, m, p, o**

Skip 2 letters, go back 1, skip 2 letters, go back 1, repeating this pattern. For example, a, skip b-c, d, c, skip d-e, f, e, skip f-g, h, g, skip h-i, j, i, etc.

(18) 1, 2, 6, 9, 10, 14, 17, 18, 22, 25, 26, 30, 33, **34, 38, 41, 42**

Add 1, add 4, add 3, add 1, add 4, add 3, repeating this pattern. For example, $1 + 1 = 2$, $2 + 4 = 6$, $6 + 3 = 9$, $9 + 1 = 10$, $10 + 4 = 14$, $14 + 3 = 17$, $17 + 1 = 18$, $18 + 4 = 22$, and $22 + 3 = 25$.

(19) 2, 5, 10, 9, 12, 24, 23, 26, 52, 51, 54, 108, 107, **110, 220, 219, 222**

Add 3, double, subtract 1, add 3, double, subtract 1, repeating this pattern. For example, $2 + 3 = 5$, $5 \times 2 = 10$, $10 - 1 = 9$, $9 + 3 = 12$, $12 \times 2 = 24$, and $24 - 1 = 23$.

(20) 8, 6, 24, 12, 10, 40, 20, 18, 72, 36, 34, 136, 68, **66, 264, 132, 130**

Subtract 2, multiply by 4, cut in half, subtract 2, multiply by 4, cut in half, repeating this pattern. For example, $8 - 2 = 6$, $6 \times 4 = 24$, $24 \div 2 = 12$, $12 - 2 = 10$, $10 \times 4 = 40$, and $40 \div 2 = 20$.

7 Digits

(1) 807, 716, 625, 534, **443, 352, 261, 170**

The first digit decreases (8, 7, 6, etc.), the middle digit increases (0, 1, 2, etc.), and the last digit decreases (7, 6, 5, etc.).

(2) 29, 47, 65, 83, 21, 49, **67, 85, 23, 41**

The first digit cycles through 2, 4, 6, 8, while the last digit cycles through 9, 7, 5, 3, 1.

(3) 122, 223, 324, 425, **526, 627, 728, 829**

The first digit increases (1, 2, 3, etc.), the middle digit is always 2, and the last digit increases (2, 3, 4, etc.).

(4) 369, 396, **639**, 693, 936, **963**, 369, **396, 639**

This sequence cycles through all 6 permutations of the digits 3, 6, and 9: 369, 396, 639, 693, 936, and 963.

(5) 5678, 5687, 5768, 5786, **5867**, 5876, 6578, **6587**, 6758, **6785, 6857**, 6875

This sequence cycles through all 12 permutations of the digits 5, 6, 7, and 8.

(6) 3456, 3465, **5436**, 5463, 6435, 6453, 3456, **3465, 5436, 5463**

The second digit is always 4. The remaining digits cycle through all 6 permutations of the digits 3, 5, and 6.

(7) d8, f7, h6, j5, **l4, n3, p2, r1**

The letter skips every other letter of the alphabet (d, skip e, f, skip g, h, skip i, etc.), while the number decreases by 1 (8, 7, 6, etc.)

(8) y3C, v5d, s7E, p9f, m1G, **j3h, g5I, d7j, a9K**

The first letter skips two letters going backward (y, skip x-w, v, skip u-t, s, skip r-q, p, etc.), the number cycles through single-digit odd numbers (1, 3, 5, 7, 9), and the last letter advances one while changing case (C, d, E, f, G, h, etc.).

(9) T8e2, r7Q4, P6E6, n5q8, L4e0, j3Q2, **H2E4, f1q6, D0e8, b9Q0**

The first letter skips one letter going backward while alternating case (T, skip S, r, skip q, P, skip O, n, skip m, L, etc.), the first number decreases by 1 (8, 7, 6, etc.) with 9 following 0, the second letter cycles through e, Q, E, and q, and the last digit cycles through single-digit even numbers (0, 2, 4, 6, 8).

Answers

(10) 24680, 24681, 24691, 24791, 25791, 35791, 35792, 35702, **35802, 36802, 46802, 46803**
Increase the 5th digit by 1, increase the 4th digit by 1, increase the 3rd digit by 1, increase the 2nd digit by 1, increase the 1st digit by 1, increase the 5th digit by 1, and so on (where increasing 9 by 1 changes it to zero). For example, 35791 changes to 35792 as the 5th digit increase from 1 to 2, 35792 changes to 35702 as the 4th digit changes from 9 to 0, and 35702 changes to 35802 as the 3rd digit increases from 7 to 8.

(11) 89, 98, 179, 188, 197, 269, 278, **287, 296, 359, 368**
These are the numbers, in order, where the digits add up to 17. For example, $8 + 9 = 17$, $9 + 8 = 17$, $1 + 7 + 9 = 17$, and $1 + 8 + 8 = 17$.

(12) 10, 11, 20, 12, 21, 30, 13, **22, 31, 40, 14**
First, write down all the two-digit numbers where the digits add up to 1 (the only answer is 10). Next, write down all the two-digit numbers in order where the digits add up to 2 (11 and 20). Next, write down all the two-digit numbers in order where the digits add up to 3 (12, 21, and 30). Next, write down all the two-digit numbers in order where the digits add up to 4 (13, 22, 31, and 40). Next, write down all the two-digit numbers in order where the digits add up to 5 (14, 23, 32, 41, and 50).

(13) 39, 57, 75, 93, 1119, **1137,** 1155, 1173, 1191, 1317, **1335, 1353, 1371**
These are the numbers, in order, composed of odd digits where the digits add up to 12. For example, $3 + 9 = 12$, $5 + 7 = 12$, $7 + 5 = 12$, $9 + 3 = 12$, $1 + 1 + 1 + 9 = 12$, and $1 + 1 + 3 + 7 = 12$.

(14) 117, 144, 171, 225, 252, 333, 414, **441**, **522**, **711**, 1116, **1125**

These are numbers with at least two repeating digits where the digits add up to 9. For example, $1 + 1 + 7 = 9$, $1 + 4 + 4 = 9$, $1 + 7 + 1 = 9$, and $2 + 2 + 5 = 9$. (At least two of the digits must be the same.)

(15) 13, 35, 57, 79, 135, 357, 579, **1357**, **3579**, **13579**

These numbers have odd digits increasing in order. For example, 357 has odd digits increasing in order.

(16) 892, 128, 783, 237, 674, 346, 565, 455, **456**, **564**, **347**, **673**

Two sequences are merged together. One is 892, 783, 674, etc., where the first digit decreases by 1 (8, 7, 6, etc.), the middle digit decreases by 1 (9, 8, 7, etc.), and the last digit increases by 1 (2, 3, 4, etc.). The other is 128, 237, 346, etc., where the first digit increases by 1 (1, 2, 3, etc.), the middle digit increases by 1 (2, 3, 4, etc.), and the last digit decreases by 1 (8, 7, 6, etc.).

(17) **Act**, Atc, **Cat**, Cta, Tac, Tca, **Act**, Atc, **Cat**, Cta

This sequence cycles through the 6 permutations of the letters a, c, and t, where the first letter is capitalized.

(18) **TOPS**, TOSP, TPOS, TPSO, TSOP, **TSPO**, SOPT, SOTP, **SPOT**, SPTO, **STOP**, STPO

This sequence cycles through 12 of the 24 permutations of the letters T, O, P, and S.

(19) bit, diq, fin, hik, jih, **lie**, **nib**, piy, **riv**, **tis**, vip

The first letter skips every other letter (b, skip c, d, skip e, f, skip g, etc.), the middle letter is always i, and the last letter skips 2 letters going backward (t, skip s-r, q, skip p-o, n, skip m-l, k, skip j-i, etc.), where a follows z (going y, skip z-a, b).

(20) Ae, Bd, Cc, Db, Ea, Aad, Abc, **Acb, Ada,Bac, Bbb**
Let a = 1, b = 2, c = 3, d = 4, and e = 5. Using these numerical values, each group of letters adds up to 6. For example, A + e = 1 + 5 = 6, B + d = 2 + 4 = 6, C + c = 3 + 3 = 6, Aad = 1 + 1 + 4 = 6, Bac = 2 + 1 + 3 = 6, and Bbb = 2 + 2 + 2 = 6.

(21) 123, 342, 534, 456, 675, 867, 789, 908, 190, 012, 231, **423, 345, 564, 756**
Each number consists of 3 consecutive digits. The first number has the digits in order, the second number has the smallest digit last and the largest digit in the middle, and the third number has the smallest digit in the middle and the largest digit first. This pattern repeats over and over.

8 Prime Numbers

(1) 29, 31, 37, 41, 43, **47, 53, 59, 61**
These prime numbers appear in order. Note that 33 = 3 × 11, 35 = 5 × 7, 39 = 3 × 13, 45 = 3 × 3 × 5, 49 = 7 × 7, 51 = 3 × 17, 55 = 5 × 11, and 57 = 3 × 19.

(2) 4, 6, 8, 9, 10, 12, 14, 15, **16, 18, 20, 21**
These are the non-prime numbers. That is, the prime numbers 2, 3, 5, 7, 11, 13, 17, and 19 have been skipped.

(3) **97, 89, 83**, 79, **73**, 71, **67**, 61
These prime numbers are in reverse order. Note that 95 = 5 × 19, 93 = 3 × 31, 91 = 7 × 13, 87 = 3 × 29, 85 =

$5 \times 17, 81 = 3 \times 3 \times 3 \times 3, 77 = 7 \times 11, 75 = 3 \times 5 \times 5,$
$69 = 3 \times 23, 65 = 5 \times 13,$ and $63 = 3 \times 3 \times 7.$

(4) 2, 3, 7, 11, 17, 19, 29, 31, 41, **43, 53, 59, 67**

Skip every third prime number: 2, 3, skip 5, 7, 11, skip 13, 17, 19, skip 23, 29, 31, skip 37, 41, etc.

(5) 3, 4, 6, 8, 12, 14, **18, 20, 24, 30**

Add 1 to each prime number. For example, $2 + 1 = 3, 3 + 1 = 4, 5 + 1 = 6, 7 + 1 = 8, 11 + 1 = 12,$ and $13 + 1 = 14.$

(6) 11, 31, 41, 61, 71, **101, 131, 151, 181**

These prime numbers end with 1. Note that $21 = 3 \times 7,$ $51 = 3 \times 17, 81 = 3 \times 3 \times 3 \times 3, 91 = 7 \times 13, 111 = 3 \times 37, 121 = 11 \times 11, 141 = 3 \times 47, 161 = 7 \times 23,$ and $171 = 3 \times 3 \times 19.$

(7) 3, 5, 7, 23, 29, 41, 43, 47, **61, 67, 83, 89,** 113

These are the prime numbers where the digits add up to an odd number. For example, 23's digits add up to 5, 47's digits add up to 11, and 113's digits add up to 5.

(8) 9, 21, 39, 57, 87, 111, **129, 159, 183, 213**

Every other prime number is tripled: Skip 2, $3 \times 3 = 9,$ skip 5, $7 \times 3 = 21,$ skip 11, $13 \times 3 = 39,$ skip 17, $19 \times 3 = 57.$

(9) 21, 25, 33, 37, 45, 57, 61, **73, 81, 85, 93**

Multiple the prime number by 2 and then subtract 1. For example, $11 \times 2 - 1 = 22 - 1 = 21, 13 \times 2 - 1 = 26 - 1 = 25, 17 \times 2 - 1 = 34 - 1 = 33,$ and $19 \times 2 - 1 = 38 - 1 = 37.$

(10) 4, 10, 22, 34, 46, 62, **82, 94, 118, 134**

Double every other prime number: $2 \times 2 = 4,$ skip 3, $5 \times 2 = 10,$ skip 7, $11 \times 2 = 22,$ skip 13, $17 \times 2 = 34,$ etc.

(11) 101, 103, 107, 109, 113, **127, 131, 137, 139**

These prime numbers appear in order.

(12) 102, 103, 105, 107, 111, 113, **117**, **119**, **123**, **129**

Add 100 to each prime number: $2 + 100 = 102, 3 + 100 = 103, 5 + 100 = 105, 7 + 100 = 107, 11 + 100 = 111$, etc.

(13) 3, 5, 5, 7, 11, 13, 17, 19, 29, 31, 41, 43, **59**, **61**, **71**, **73**

These are pairs of consecutive odd-numbered primes. For example, 3 and 5 are consecutive odd-numbered primes. Another example is 5 and 7. Another pair is 11 and 13.

(14) 2, 3, 5, 7, 11, 23, 29, 41, 43, 47, 61, 67, 83, **89**, **101**, **113**, **131**

These are the prime numbers where the digits add up to a prime number. For example, the 1 and 1 of 11 add up to 2, the 2 and 3 of 23 add up to 5, the 2 and 9 of 29 add up to 11, the 4 and 1 of 41 add up to 5, and the 4 and 3 of 43 add up to 7.

9 Fibonacci Inspired

(1) 2, 2, 4, 6, 10, 16, **26**, **42**, **68**, **110**

Add consecutive numbers: $2 + 2 = 4, 2 + 4 = 6, 4 + 6 = 10, 6 + 10 = 16, 10 + 16 = 26$, etc.

(2) 1, 3, **4**, 7, 11, 18, 29, 47, **76**, **123**

Add consecutive numbers: $1 + 3 = 4, 3 + 4 = 7, 4 + 7 = 11, 7 + 11 = 18$, etc.

(3) 6, **9**, 15, **24**, 39, 63, **102**, 165, **267**, 432

Add consecutive numbers: $6 + 9 = 15, 9 + 15 = 24, 15 + 24 = 39, 24 + 39 = 63$, etc.

(4) 309, 191, 118, 73, 45, 28, **17**, **11**, **6**, **5**

Subtract consecutive numbers: $309 - 191 = 118, 191 - 118 = 73, 118 - 73 = 45$, etc.

(5) 1, 2, 2, 4, 8, 32, **256, 8192, 2097152**

Multiply consecutive numbers: $1 \times 2 = 2, 2 \times 2 = 4, 2 \times 4 = 8, 4 \times 8 = 32$, etc.

(6) 1, 2, 5, 13, 34, 89, 233, **610, 1597, 4181, 10946**

Skip every other number of the Fibonacci sequence: 1, skip 1, 2, skip 3, 5, skip 8, 13, skip 21, etc.

(7) 1, 1, 2, 4, 7, 13, 24, 44, 81, 149, **274, 504, 927, 1705**

Add the 3 previous numbers: $1 + 1 + 2 = 4, 1 + 2 + 4 = 7, 2 + 4 + 7 = 13, 4 + 7 + 13 = 24$, etc.

(8) 2, 3, 3, 4, 5, 7, 10, 15, 23, 36, **57, 91, 146, 235**

Add consecutive numbers and subtract 2: $2 + 3 - 2 = 3, 3 + 3 - 2 = 4, 3 + 4 - 2 = 5, 4 + 5 - 2 = 7, 5 + 7 - 2 = 10$, etc.

(9) 1, 3, 5, 9, 15, 25, 41, 67, 109, 177, **287, 465, 753, 1219**

Add consecutive numbers and add 1: $1 + 3 + 1 = 5, 3 + 5 + 1 = 9, 5 + 9 + 1 = 15, 9 + 15 + 1 = 25, 15 + 25 + 1 = 41$, etc.

(10) 0, 1, 2, 2, 3, 5, 7, 10, 15, 22, 32, 47, 69, 101, **148, 217, 318, 466**

Add the 3 previous numbers and subtract the middle of those three numbers. Put another way, add the previous number to the number two places before it. For example, $0 + 1 + 2 - 1 = 2$ (or simply $0 + 2 = 2$), $1 + 2 + 2 - 2 = 3$ (or $1 + 2 = 3$), $2 + 2 + 3 - 2 = 5$ (or $2 + 3 = 5$), $2 + 3 + 5 - 3 = 7$ (or $2 + 5 = 7$), $3 + 5 + 7 - 5 = 10$ (or $3 + 7 = 10$), $5 + 7 + 10 - 7 = 15$ (or $5 + 10 = 15$), and $7 + 10 + 15 - 10 = 22$ (or $7 + 15 = 22$).

10 Roman Numerals

(1) II, IV, **VI**, VIII, X, **XII**, **XIV**, XVI, **XVIII**, XX
These are even numbers (2, 4, 6, etc.).

(2) III, VI, XII, XXIV, XLVIII, **XCVI**, **CXCII**, **CCCLXXXIV**, **DCCLXVIII**
Double each number (3 × 2 = 6, 6 × 2 = 12, 12 × 2 = 24, 24 × 2 = 48, etc.).

(3) CVI, CV, CIV, CIII, CII, CI, **C**, **XCIX**, **XCVIII**, **XCVII**
Count backwards (106, 105, 104, 103, 102, etc.). Note that 99 is correctly written as XCIX and not IC.

(4) XXV, L, LXXV, C, CXXV, CL, **CLXXV**, **CC**, **CCXXV**, **CCL**
Count by 25 (25, 50, 75, 100, 125, etc.).

(5) C, CC, CCC, CD, D, DC, **DCC**, **DCCC**, **CM**, **M**
Count by 100 (100, 200, 300, 400, 500, etc.).

(6) MCMLX, MCMLXV, MCMLXX, MCMLXXV, MCMLXXX, MCMLXXXV, **MCMXC**, **MCMXCV**, **MM**, **MMV**
Count by 5 (1960, 1965, 1970, 1975, 1980, etc.).

(7) DLXX, DLX, DL, DXL, DXXX, DXX, **DX**, **D**, **CDXC**, **CDLXXX**
Subtract 10 (570, 560, 550, 540, 530, etc.).

(8) IX, VII, XIV, XII, XIX, XVII, XXIV, XXII, **XXIX**, **XXVII**, **XXXIV**, **XXXII**
Subtract 2, add 7, subtract 2, add 7, repeating this pattern (9 – 2 = 7, 7 + 7 = 14, 14 – 2 = 12, 12 + 7 = 19, 19 – 2 = 17, 17 + 7 = 24, etc.).

(9) II, VI, III, IX, VI, XVIII, XV, XLV, XLII, **CXXVI**, **CXXIII**, **CCCLXIX**, **CCCLXVI**
Multiply by 3, subtract 3, multiply by 3, subtract 3, repeating this pattern (2 × 3 = 6, 6 – 3 = 3, 3 × 3 = 9, 9 – 3 = 6, 6 × 3 = 18, 18 – 3= 15, etc.).

(10) VII, IX, XII, XVI, XXI, XXVII, **XXXIV, XLII, LI, LXI**
Add 2, add 3, add 4, add 5, etc. ($7 + 2 = 9, 9 + 3 = 12$, $12 + 4 = 16, 16 + 5 = 21, 21 + 6 = 27$, etc.).

(11) II, IV, VI, IX, XI, XV, XX, XL, LI, **LV, LX, XC, CI**
These are the Roman numerals that can be made with exactly two letters, in numerical order.

(12) CC, CD, CI, CL, CM, CV, CX, DC, DI, **DL, DV, DX, II**
These are the Roman numerals that can be made with exactly two letters, in alphabetical order.

(13) III, V, IX, XVII, XXXIII, LXV, CXXIX, **CCLVII, DXIII, MXXV, MMXLIX**
Multiply the previous number by 2 and subtract 1: ($2 \times 3 - 1 = 5, 2 \times 5 - 1 = 9, 2 \times 9 - 1 = 17, 2 \times 17 - 1 = 33$, $2 \times 33 - 1 = 65$, etc.).

(14) I, I, II, III, V, VIII, XIII, XXI, **XXXIV, LV, LXXXIX, CXLIV**
This is the Fibonacci sequence (Chapter 9): 1, 1, 2, 3, 5, 8, 13, 21, etc.

(15) II, III, V, VII, XI, XIII, XVII, **XIX, XXIII, XXIX, XXXI**
These are prime numbers (Chapter 8): 2, 3, 5, 7, 11, 13, 17, etc.

11 Powers

(1) **1**, 4, 9, 16, **25**, 36, **49, 64**
Square consecutive numbers: $1^2 = 1, 2^2 = 4, 3^2 = 9, 4^2 = 16, 5^2 = 25$, etc.

(2) 1, **2, 4**, 8, 16, 32, 64, **128, 256**
Raise 2 to the next power: $2^0 = 1, 2^1 = 2, 2^2 = 4, 2^3 = 8$, $2^4 = 16, 2^5 = 32$, etc.

(3) 1, 100, 10000, 1000000, **100000000**, **10000000000, 1000000000000, 100000000000000**

Raise 10 to the next even power: $10^0 = 1$, $10^2 = 100$, $10^4 = 10000$, $10^6 = 100000$, etc.

(4) 1, 16, 81, 256, 625, 1296, **2401, 4096, 6561, 10000**

These are powers of 4: $1^4 = 1$, $2^4 = 16$, $3^4 = 81$, $4^4 = 256$, $5^4 = 625$, etc.

(5) 4, 16, 36, 64, 100, 144, **196, 256, 324, 400**

Square even numbers: $2^2 = 4$, $4^2 = 16$, $6^2 = 36$, $8^2 = 64$, $10^2 = 100$, etc.

(6) 1, 4, 27, 256, 3125, **46656, 823543**

Raise each number to the power of itself: $1^1 = 1$, $2^2 = 4$, $3^3 = 27$, $4^4 = 256$, $5^5 = 3125$, etc.

(7) 1, 16, 256, 4096, **65536, 1048576**

Raise 4 to the next even power: $4^0 = 1$, $4^2 = 16$, $4^4 = 256$, $4^6 = 4096$, $4^8 = 65536$, etc.

(8) 0, 3, 8, 15, 24, 35, **48, 63, 80, 99**

These are squares minus one: $1^2 - 1 = 0$, $2^2 - 1 = 3$, $3^2 - 1 = 8$, $4^2 - 1 = 15$, $5^2 - 1 = 24$, etc.

(9) 4, 9, 25, 49, 121, 169, **289, 361, 529, 841**

Square prime numbers (see Chapter 8): $2^2 = 4$, $3^2 = 9$, $5^2 = 25$, $7^2 = 49$, $11^2 = 121$, etc.

(10) 2, 8, 18, 32, 50, 72, **98, 128, 162, 200**

Double each square: $2 \times 1^2 = 2$, $2 \times 2^2 = 8$, $2 \times 3^2 = 18$, $2 \times 4^2 = 32$, $2 \times 5^2 = 50$, etc.

12 Factorials

(1) 1, 6, 120, 5040, 362880, **39916800, 6227020800**

Skip every other factorial: $1! = 1$, skip $2!$, $3! = 6$, skip $4!$, $5! = 120$, skip 6, $7! = 5040$, etc.

(2) $1, 3, 15, 105, 945, \mathbf{10395}, \mathbf{135135}, \mathbf{2027025}, \mathbf{34459425}$

These are double factorials with odd numbers: $1!! = 1$, $3!! = 3 \times 1 = 3$, $5!! = 5 \times 3 \times 1 = 15$, $7!! = 7 \times 5 \times 3 \times 1 = 105$, $9!! = 9 \times 7 \times 5 \times 3 \times 1 = 945$, etc.

(3) $1, 1, 2, 3, 8, 15, 48, 105, 384, \mathbf{945}, \mathbf{3840}, \mathbf{10395}, \mathbf{46080}$

Each number starts with a factorial and divides by the previous number: 1, $1! \div 1 = 1$, $2! \div 1 = 2$, $3! \div 2 = 3$, $4! \div 3 = 8$, $5! \div 8 = 15$, $6! \div 15 = 48$, $7! \div 48 = 105$, $8! \div 105 = 384$, etc.

(4) $2, 2, 4, 12, 48, 240, \mathbf{1440}, \mathbf{10080}, \mathbf{80640}, \mathbf{725760}$

Multiply each factorial by two: $(0!) \times 2 = 1 \times 2 = 2$, $(1!) \times 2 = 1 \times 2 = 2$, $(2!) \times 2 = 2 \times 2 = 4$, $(3!) \times 2 = 6 \times 2 = 12$, $(4!) \times 2 = 24 \times 2 = 48$, etc.

(5) $1, 1, 4, 36, 576, 14400, \mathbf{518400}, \mathbf{25401600}$

Square each factorial: $(0!)^2 = 1^2 = 1$, $(1!)^2 = 1^2 = 1$, $(2!)^2 = 2^2 = 4$, $(3!)^2 = 6^2 = 36$, $(4!)^2 = 24^2 = 576$, etc.

(6) $1, 7, 21, 35, 35, \mathbf{21}, \mathbf{7}, \mathbf{1}$

This sequence is made from the combination formula for $N = 7$:

$$\frac{7!}{7!\,0!} = 1 \qquad \frac{7!}{6!\,1!} = 7 \qquad \frac{7!}{5!\,2!} = 21 \qquad \frac{7!}{4!\,3!} = 35$$

$$\frac{7!}{3!\,4!} = 35 \qquad \frac{7!}{2!\,5!} = 21 \qquad \frac{7!}{1!\,6!} = 7 \qquad \frac{7!}{0!\,7!} = 1$$

(7) $1, 9, 36, \mathbf{84}, \mathbf{126}, \mathbf{126}, \mathbf{84}, 36, 9, 1$

This sequence is made from the combination formula for $N = 9$:

$$\frac{9!}{9!\,0!} = 1 \qquad \frac{9!}{8!\,1!} = 9 \qquad \frac{9!}{7!\,2!} = 36 \qquad \frac{9!}{6!\,3!} = 84 \qquad \frac{9!}{5!\,4!} = 126$$

$$\frac{9!}{4!\,5!} = 126 \qquad \frac{9!}{3!\,6!} = 84 \qquad \frac{9!}{2!\,7!} = 36 \qquad \frac{9!}{1!\,8!} = 9 \qquad \frac{9!}{0!\,9!} = 1$$

(8) $1, 4, 10, 20, 35, 56, \mathbf{84}, \mathbf{120}, \mathbf{165}, \mathbf{220}$

One way to make this sequence is to read along a

diagonal of Pascal's triangle, as illustrated below:

$$x + y$$
$$x^2 + 2xy + y^2$$
$$x^3 + 3x^2y + 3xy^2 + y^3$$
$$x^4 + 4x^3y + 6x^2y^2 + 4xy^3 + y^4$$
$$x^5 + 5x^4y + 10x^3y^2 + 10x^2y^3 + 5xy^4 + y^5$$
$$x^6 + 6x^5y + 15x^4y^2 + 20x^3y^3 + 15x^2y^4 + 6xy^5 + y^6$$
$$x^7 + 7x^6y + 21x^5y^2 + 35x^4y^3 + 35x^3y^4 + 21x^2y^5 + 7xy^6 + y^7$$
$$x^8 + 8x^7y + 28x^6y^2 + 56x^5y^3 + 70x^4y^4 + 56x^3y^5 + 28x^2y^6 + 8xy^7 + y^8$$

Another way to make this sequence is to add 3, add 6, add 10, add 15, add 21, etc. (The pattern 3, 6, 10, 15, 21, etc. is made by adding 3, 4, 5, 6, etc.) For example, $1 + 3 = 4, 4 + 6 = 10, 10 + 10 = 20, 20 + 15 = 35$, and $35 + 21 = 56$.

(9) 2, 3, 8, 30, 144, 840, 5760, **45360, 403200, 3991680, 43545600**

Add consecutive factorials: $2! + 1! = 3, 3! + 2! = 8, 4! + 3! = 30, 5! + 4! = 144, 6! + 5! = 840$, etc.

(10) 3628800, 1814400, 604800, 151200, 30240, 5040, **720, 90, 10, 1**

This sequence is made by dividing 10! by a smaller factorial: $10! / 1! = 3628800, 10! / 2! = 1814400, 10! / 3! = 604800, 10! / 4! = 151200, 10! / 5! = 30240$, etc.

13 Negative Numbers

(1) –28, –24, –20, –16, –12, –8, **–4, 0, 4, 8**

Add 4: $-28 + 4 = -24, -24 + 4 = -20, -20 + 4 = -16$, etc.

(2) –2, 4, –8, 16, –32, 64, **–128, 256, –512, 1024**

Multiply by –2: $-2 \times (-2) = 4, 4 \times (-2) = -8, -8 \times (-2) = 16, 16 \times (-2) = -32$, etc.

(3) 3, –5, 7, –7, 11, –9, 15, –11, **19, –13, 23, –15**

Two sequences are merged together. One sequence

adds 4 $(3 + 4 = 7, 7 + 4 = 11, 11 + 4 = 15$, etc.), while the other sequence subtracts 2 $(-5 - 2 = -7, -7 - 2 = -9, -9 - 2 = -11$, etc.): The sequence 7, 11, 15, 19, 23, etc. is mixed with the sequence $-5, -7, -9, -11, -13$, etc.

(4) $-57, 43, -42, 35, -27, 27, -12, 19, \mathbf{3}, \mathbf{11}, \mathbf{18}, \mathbf{3}$

Two sequences are merged together. One sequence adds 15 $(-57 + 15 = -42, -42 + 15 = -27, -27 + 15 = -12$, etc.), while the other sequence subtracts 8 $(43 - 8 = 35, 35 - 8 = 27, 27 - 8 = 19$, etc.): The sequence $-57, -42, -27, -12$, etc. is mixed with the sequence 43, 35, 27, 19, etc.

(5) 1, -3, -15, 45, 33, -99, -111, 333, 321, $\mathbf{-963}$, $\mathbf{-975}, \mathbf{2925}, \mathbf{2913}$

Multiply by -3, subtract 12, multiply by -3, subtract 12, repeating this pattern: $1 \times (-3) = -3, -3 - 12 = -15, -15 \times (-3) = 45, 45 - 12 = 33, 33 \times (-3) = -99, -99 - 12 = -111$, etc.

(6) 0, 1, -1, 2, -3, 5, -8, 13, -21, $\mathbf{34}, \mathbf{-55}, \mathbf{89}, \mathbf{-144}$

Make every other element of the Fibonacci sequence negative (Chapter 9).

(7) -3, 4, -4, 3, -4, 4, -3, 4, -4, 3, -4, $\mathbf{4}, \mathbf{-3}, \mathbf{4}, \mathbf{-4}$

Repeat the pattern 3, 4, 4, 3, 4, 4 over and over, making every other number negative.

(8) 20, 19, 17, 14, 10, 5, $\mathbf{-1}, \mathbf{-8}, \mathbf{-16}, \mathbf{-25}$

Subtract 1, subtract 2, subtract 3, subtract 4, subtract 5, etc.: $20 - 1 = 19, 19 - 2 = 17, 17 - 3 = 14, 14 - 4 = 10, 10 - 5 = 5, 5 - 6 = -1, -1 - 7 = -8$, etc.

(9) 3, 9, -9, 27, -27, -27, 81, -81, -81, -81, 243, $-$243, -243, $\mathbf{-243}, \mathbf{-243}, \mathbf{729}, \mathbf{-729}$

This pattern involves powers of 3. $3^1, 3^2, -(3^2), 3^3, -(3^3), -(3^3), 3^4, -(3^4), -(3^4), -(3^4), 3^5, -(3^5), -(3^5), -(3^5), -(3^5),$

etc. There is one more negative number each time the power increases.

(10) –6, –9, –15, –21, –33, –39, –51, –57, –69, **–87, –93, –111, –123**

These are prime numbers (Chapter 8) multiplied by –3:

$2 \times (-3) = -6$, $3 \times (-3) = -9$, $5 \times (-3) = -15$, $7 \times (-3) = -21$, $11 \times (-3) = -33$, $13 \times (-3) = -39$ etc.

14 Fractions

(1) $\frac{2}{3}, \frac{4}{5}, \frac{6}{7}, \frac{8}{9}, \frac{10}{11}, \frac{12}{13}, \frac{14}{15}, \frac{16}{17}, \frac{18}{19}$

Increase each numerator and denominator by 2. For example, the 2 of $\frac{2}{3}$ becomes $2 + 2 = 4$ and the 3 of $\frac{2}{3}$ becomes $3 + 2 = 5$, making $\frac{4}{5}$. Similarly, $\frac{6}{7}$ turns into $\frac{8}{9}$, since $6 + 2 = 8$ and $7 + 2 = 9$.

(2) $\frac{1}{3}, \frac{5}{6}, \frac{1}{12}, \frac{23}{24}, \frac{1}{48}, \frac{95}{96}, \frac{1}{192}, \frac{383}{384}, \frac{1}{768}, \frac{1535}{1536}$

Double the denominator (3, 6, 12, 24, etc.). The numerator alternates between 1 and the denominator minus 1.

(3) $\frac{1}{4}, \frac{6}{7}, \frac{3}{8}, \frac{10}{11}, \frac{5}{12}, \frac{14}{15}, \frac{7}{16}, \frac{18}{19}, \frac{9}{20}, \frac{22}{23}, \frac{11}{24}, \frac{26}{27}$

For the numerator, add 5, divide by 2, add 7, divide by 2, add 9, divide by 2, add 11, divide by 2, repeating this pattern ($1 + 5 = 6$, $6 \div 2 = 3$, $3 + 7 = 10$, $10 \div 2 = 5$, $5 + 9 = 14$, $14 \div 2 = 7$, $7 + 11 = 18$, etc.). For the denominator, add 3, add 1, add 3, add 1, repeating this pattern ($4 + 3 = 7$, $7 + 1 = 8$, $8 + 3 = 11$, $11 + 1 = 12$, etc.).

(4) $\frac{1}{16}, \frac{1}{8}, \frac{3}{16}, \frac{1}{4}, \frac{5}{16}, \frac{3}{8}, \frac{7}{16}, \frac{1}{2}, \frac{9}{16}, \frac{5}{8}, \frac{11}{16}$

Add $\frac{1}{16}$: $\frac{1}{16} + \frac{1}{16} = \frac{1}{8}$, $\frac{1}{8} + \frac{1}{16} = \frac{3}{16}$, $\frac{3}{16} + \frac{1}{16} = \frac{1}{4}$, etc.

(5) 0.5, 0.25, 0.125, 0.0625, 0.03125, 0.015625, **0.0078125, 0.00390625, 0.001953125, 0.0009765625**

Divide by 2: $0.5 \div 2 = 0.25$, $0.25 \div 2 = 0.125$, $0.125 \div 2 = 0.0625$, etc.

(6) $\frac{1}{2}, 1\frac{1}{2}, 4\frac{1}{2}, 13\frac{1}{2}, 40\frac{1}{2}, 121\frac{1}{2}, \mathbf{364\frac{1}{2}, 1093\frac{1}{2}, 3280\frac{1}{2}, 9841\frac{1}{2}}$

Add 3^0, add 3^1, add 3^2, add 3^3, add 3^4, etc.:

$$\frac{1}{2} + 1 = 1\frac{1}{2} \qquad 1\frac{1}{2} + 3 = 4\frac{1}{2} \qquad 4\frac{1}{2} + 9 = 13\frac{1}{2}$$

$$13\frac{1}{2} + 27 = 40\frac{1}{2} \qquad 40\frac{1}{2} + 81 = 121\frac{1}{2} \qquad 121\frac{1}{2} + 243 = 364\frac{1}{2}$$

(7) $\frac{1}{5}, \frac{13}{15}, 1\frac{8}{15}, 2\frac{1}{5}, 2\frac{13}{15}, 3\frac{8}{15}, 4\frac{1}{5}, \mathbf{4\frac{13}{15}, 5\frac{8}{15}, 6\frac{1}{5}, 6\frac{13}{15}}$

Add $\frac{2}{3}$: $\frac{1}{5} + \frac{2}{3} = \frac{13}{15}, \frac{13}{15} + \frac{2}{3} = \frac{23}{15}$ (or 1 and $\frac{8}{15}$), $\frac{23}{15} + \frac{2}{3} = \frac{11}{5}$

(or 2 and $\frac{1}{5}$), $\frac{11}{5} + \frac{2}{3} = \frac{43}{15}$ (or 2 and $\frac{13}{15}$), $\frac{43}{15} + \frac{2}{3} = \frac{53}{15}$ (or 3

and $\frac{8}{15}$), etc.

(8) $\frac{1}{12}, \frac{1}{6}, \frac{1}{4}, \frac{1}{3}, \frac{5}{12}, \frac{1}{2}, \frac{7}{12}, \frac{2}{3}, \frac{3}{4}, \frac{5}{6}$

Add $\frac{1}{12}$: $\frac{1}{12} + \frac{1}{12} = \frac{1}{6}, \frac{1}{6} + \frac{1}{12} = \frac{1}{4}, \frac{1}{4} + \frac{1}{12} = \frac{1}{3}, \frac{1}{3} + \frac{1}{12} = \frac{5}{12}$, etc.

(9) $\frac{1}{2}, \frac{1}{3}, \frac{5}{6}, 1\frac{1}{6}, 2, 3\frac{1}{6}, 5\frac{1}{6}, 8\frac{1}{3}, 13\frac{1}{2}, \mathbf{21\frac{5}{6}, 35\frac{1}{3}, 57\frac{1}{6}, 92\frac{1}{2}}$

Add consecutive fractions (like the Fibonacci sequence described in Chapter 9): $\frac{1}{2} + \frac{1}{3} = \frac{5}{6}, \frac{1}{3} + \frac{5}{6} = \frac{7}{6}$ (or 1 and $\frac{1}{6}$),

$\frac{5}{6} + \frac{7}{6} = 2, \frac{7}{6} + 2 = \frac{19}{6}$ (or 3 and $\frac{1}{6}$), $2 + \frac{19}{6} = \frac{31}{6}$ (or 5 and $\frac{1}{6}$), etc.

(10) $4\frac{3}{7}, 5\frac{5}{9}, 6\frac{7}{11}, 9\frac{7}{13}, 8\frac{11}{15}, 13\frac{9}{17}, 10\frac{15}{19}, 17\frac{11}{21}, \mathbf{12\frac{19}{23}},$

$\mathbf{21\frac{13}{25}, 14\frac{23}{27}, 25\frac{15}{29}}$

The denominators are consecutive odd numbers (7, 9, 11, 13, etc.). Two more patterns alternate between the numerators and whole numbers. One pattern is 4, 5, 6, 7, 8, etc. with the first whole number, second numerator, third whole number, fourth numerator, etc. The other is 3, 5, 7, 9, 11, etc. with the first numerator, second whole number, third numerator, fourth whole number, etc.

(11) 0.125, 0.5, 0.875, 1.25, 1.625, **2, 2.375, 2.75, 3.125**
Add 0.375: 0.125 + 0.375 = 0.5, 0.5 + 0.375 = 0.875, 0.875 + 0.375 = 1.25, etc.

(12) $\frac{2}{5}, \frac{3}{7}, \frac{5}{11}, \frac{7}{15}, \frac{11}{23}, \frac{13}{27}, \frac{17}{35}, \mathbf{\frac{19}{39}}, \mathbf{\frac{23}{47}}, \mathbf{\frac{29}{59}}, \mathbf{\frac{31}{63}}$

The numerators are prime numbers (2, 3, 5, 7, 11, 13, 17, etc.). The denominator is twice the numerator plus 1: $2 \times 2 + 1 = 5$, $3 \times 2 + 1 = 7$, $5 \times 2 + 1 = 11$, $7 \times 2 + 1 = 15$, $11 \times 2 + 1 = 23$, etc.

(13) $\frac{1}{2}, \frac{1}{3}, \frac{2}{9}, \frac{4}{27}, \frac{8}{81}, \frac{16}{243}, \frac{32}{729}, \mathbf{\frac{64}{2187}}, \mathbf{\frac{128}{6561}}, \mathbf{\frac{256}{19683}}$

Multiply by $\frac{2}{3}$: $\frac{1}{2} \times \frac{2}{3} = \frac{1}{3}, \frac{1}{3} \times \frac{2}{3} = \frac{2}{9}, \frac{2}{9} \times \frac{2}{3} = \frac{4}{27}$, etc.

(14) $\frac{1}{4}, \frac{9}{16}, \frac{25}{36}, \frac{49}{64}, \frac{81}{100}, \mathbf{\frac{121}{144}}, \mathbf{\frac{169}{196}}, \mathbf{\frac{225}{256}}, \mathbf{\frac{289}{324}}$

The numerators are odd numbers squared ($1^2 = 1$, $3^2 = 9$, $5^2 = 25$, $7^2 = 49$, etc.). The denominators are even numbers squared ($2^2 = 4$, $4^2 = 16$, $6^2 = 36$, $8^2 = 64$, etc.).

(15) $1, 2, 1\frac{1}{2}, 1\frac{1}{3}, 1, \frac{3}{4}, \frac{7}{13}, \frac{8}{21}, \frac{9}{34}, \mathbf{\frac{2}{11}}, \mathbf{\frac{11}{89}}, \mathbf{\frac{1}{12}}, \mathbf{\frac{13}{233}}$

The numerators are integers (1, 2, 3, etc.). The denominators are elements of the Fibonacci sequence described in Chapter 9 (1, 1, 2, 3, 5, 8, 13, etc.). The sequence is:

$\frac{1}{1} = 1$ $\qquad$ $\frac{2}{1} = 2$ $\qquad$ $\frac{3}{2} = 1\frac{1}{2}$ $\qquad$ $\frac{4}{3} = 1\frac{1}{3}$

$\frac{5}{5} = 1$ $\qquad$ $\frac{6}{8} = \frac{3}{4}$ $\qquad$ $\frac{7}{13}$ $\qquad$ $\frac{8}{21}$

(16) $\frac{1}{2}, \frac{1}{6}, \frac{5}{12}, \frac{1}{12}, \frac{1}{3}, 0, \frac{1}{4}, -\frac{1}{12}, \frac{1}{6}, -\frac{1}{6}, \frac{1}{12}, -\frac{1}{4}, 0, -\frac{1}{3}, -\frac{1}{12}$

Two sequences are merged together. Each sequence involves subtracting $\frac{1}{12}$. The first sequence is: $\frac{1}{2} - \frac{1}{12} = \frac{5}{12}$, $\frac{5}{12} - \frac{1}{12} = \frac{1}{3}$, $\frac{1}{3} - \frac{1}{12} = \frac{1}{4}$, $\frac{1}{4} - \frac{1}{12} = \frac{1}{6}$, etc. The second sequence is $\frac{1}{6} - \frac{1}{12} = \frac{1}{12}$, $\frac{1}{12} - \frac{1}{12} = 0$, $0 - \frac{1}{12} = -\frac{1}{12}$, $-\frac{1}{12} - \frac{1}{12} = -\frac{1}{6}$, etc.

(17) $0.\overline{5}, 1, 1.\overline{4}, 1.\overline{8}, 2.\overline{3}, 2.\overline{7}, 3.\overline{2}, 3.\overline{6}, 4.\overline{1}, 4.\overline{5}, 5, 5.\overline{4}$

Add $0.\overline{4}$. For example: $0.\overline{5} + 0.\overline{4} = 1$, $1 + 0.\overline{4} = 1.\overline{4}$, $1.\overline{4} + 0.\overline{4} = 1.\overline{8}$, and $1.\overline{8} + 0.\overline{4} = 2.\overline{3}$. Note: The bar over a digit indicates a repeating decimal. For example, $0.\overline{5} = 0.55555555555555555555555555555555555555...$

(18) $\frac{1}{3}, \frac{1}{2}, \frac{3}{4}, 1\frac{1}{8}, 1\frac{11}{16}, 2\frac{17}{32}, 3\frac{51}{64}, 5\frac{89}{128}, 8\frac{139}{256}, 12\frac{417}{512}$

Multiply by $\frac{3}{2}$: $\frac{1}{3} \times \frac{3}{2} = \frac{1}{2}$, $\frac{1}{2} \times \frac{3}{2} = \frac{3}{4}$, $\frac{3}{4} \times \frac{3}{2} = \frac{9}{8}$ (or 1 and $\frac{1}{8}$), $\frac{9}{8} \times \frac{3}{2} = \frac{27}{16}$ (or 1 and $\frac{11}{16}$), etc.

(19) $\frac{1}{4}, 0.5, 75\%, 1, 1.25, 150\%, 1\frac{3}{4}, 2, 225\%, 2\frac{1}{2}, 2.75,$ **300%, 3$\frac{1}{4}$**

Add 0.25, alternately expressing the answer as a fraction, decimal, or percentage: $\frac{1}{4} + 0.25 = 0.5$, $0.5 + 0.25 = 75\%$, $75\% + 0.25 = 1$, $1 + 0.25 = 1.25$, $1.25 + 0.25 = 150\%$, $150\% + 0.25 = \frac{7}{4}$ (or 1 and $\frac{3}{4}$), $\frac{7}{4} + 0.25 = 2$, etc.

(20) $\frac{1}{2}, \frac{1}{3}, 1\frac{1}{2}, \frac{2}{9}, 6\frac{3}{4}, \frac{8}{243}, 205\frac{1}{32}, \frac{256}{1594323}$

Divide consecutive fractions: $\frac{1}{2} \div \left(\frac{1}{3}\right) = \frac{3}{2}$ (or 1 and $\frac{1}{2}$), $\frac{1}{3} \div \left(\frac{3}{2}\right) = \frac{2}{9}, \frac{3}{2} \div \left(\frac{2}{9}\right) = \frac{27}{4}$ (or 6 and $\frac{3}{4}$), $\frac{2}{9} \div \left(\frac{27}{4}\right) = \frac{8}{243}$, etc.

15 Algebraic

(1) x^{10}, $10x^9$, $90x^8$, $720x^7$, **$5040x^6$**, **$30240x^5$**, **$151200x^4$**, **$604800x^3$**

Multiply by 10, multiply by 9, multiply by 8, multiply by 7, etc., while also dividing by x. For example:

$$x^{10} \cdot \frac{10}{x} = 10x^9 \qquad\qquad 10x^9 \cdot \frac{9}{x} = 90x^8$$

$$90x^8 \cdot \frac{8}{x} = 720x^7 \qquad\qquad 720x^7 \cdot \frac{7}{x} = 5040x^6$$

(2) 120, $120x$, $60x^2$, $20x^3$, $5x^4$, x^5, $\frac{x^6}{6}$, $\frac{x^7}{42}$, $\frac{x^8}{336}$

Divide by 1, divide by 2, divide by 3, divide by 4, etc.: $120 \div 1 = 120$, $120 \div 2 = 60$, $60 \div 3 = 20$, $20 \div 4 = 5$, $5 \div 5 = 1$, $1 \div 6 = 1/6$, etc. Also increase the power each time: $1, x, x^2, x^3, x^4$, etc.

(3) $4x$, $9x^2$, $16x^4$, $25x^8$, $36x^{16}$, **$49x^{32}$**, **$64x^{64}$**, **$81x^{128}$**, **$100x^{256}$**

The coefficients are squares ($2^2 = 4$, $3^2 = 9$, $4^2 = 16$, $5^2 = 25$, etc.) and the exponents are powers of 2 ($2^0 = 1$, $2^1 = 2$, $2^2 = 4$, $2^3 = 8$, $2^4 = 16$, etc.).

(4) 2, $3x^2$, $5x^4$, $7x^6$, $11x^8$, $13x^{10}$, $17x^{12}$, **$19x^{14}$**, **$23x^{16}$**, **$29x^{18}$**, **$31x^{20}$**

The coefficients (2, 3, 5, 7, 11, 13, etc.) are prime numbers (Chapter 8). The powers are even numbers (0, 2, 4, etc.), where $x^0 = 1$.

(5) x, $\frac{2}{x^2}$, $\frac{x^3}{6}$, $\frac{24}{x^5}$, $\frac{x^8}{120}$, $\frac{720}{x^{13}}$, $\frac{x^{21}}{5040}$, $\frac{40320}{x^{34}}$, $\frac{x^{55}}{362880}$, $\frac{3628800}{x^{89}}$

The Fibonacci sequence (1, 2, 3, 5, 8, 13, etc.) described in Chapter 9 forms the exponents. The constant is a factorial ($1! = 1$, $2! = 2$, $3! = 6$, $4! = 24$, $5! = 120$, $6! =$

720, etc.), which is defined in Chapter 12. The variable and constant alternate position between the numerator and denominator.

(6) $2x^4$, $7x^{11}$, $16x^{22}$, $29x^{37}$, $46x^{56}$, $\mathbf{67x^{79}}$, $\mathbf{92x^{106}}$, $\mathbf{121x^{137}}$, $\mathbf{154x^{172}}$

For the coefficients, add 5, add 9, add 13, add 17, etc.: $2 + 5 = 7, 7 + 9 = 16, 16 + 13 = 29, 29 + 17 = 46, 46 + 21 = 67$, etc. For the exponents, add 7, add 11, add 15, add 19, etc.: $4 + 7 = 11, 11 + 11 = 22, 22 + 15 = 37, 37 + 19 = 56, 56 + 23 = 79$, etc.

(7) $(a + 2)^3$, $(b + 4)^6$, $(c + 8)^{12}$, $(d + 16)^{24}$, $(e + 32)^{48}$, $(f + 64)^{96}$, $(g + 128)^{192}$, $(h + 256)^{384}$

Advance the letter (a, b, c, etc.), double the constant ($2, 4, 8, 16$, etc.), and double the power ($3, 6, 12, 24$, etc.).

(8) $\dfrac{x^4}{24}, \dfrac{x^3}{12}, \dfrac{x^2}{4}, x, 5, \dfrac{30}{x}, \dfrac{210}{x^2}, \dfrac{1680}{x^3}, \dfrac{15120}{x^4}$

Divide by $\dfrac{x}{2}$, divide by $\dfrac{x}{3}$, divide by $\dfrac{x}{4}$, divide by $\dfrac{x}{5}$, etc.:

$$\frac{x^4}{24} \div \frac{x}{2} = \frac{x^4}{24} \cdot \frac{2}{x} = \frac{x^3}{12}$$

$$\frac{x^3}{12} \div \frac{x}{3} = \frac{x^3}{12} \cdot \frac{3}{x} = \frac{x^2}{4}$$

$$\frac{x^2}{4} \div \frac{x}{4} = \frac{x^2}{4} \cdot \frac{4}{x} = x$$

$$x \div \frac{x}{5} = x \cdot \frac{5}{x} = 5$$

$$5 \div \frac{x}{6} = 5 \cdot \frac{6}{x} = \frac{30}{x}$$

$$\frac{30}{x} \div \frac{x}{7} = \frac{30}{x} \cdot \frac{7}{x} = \frac{210}{x^2}$$

(9) 2^a, c^4, 8^e, g^{16}, 32^i, $\mathbf{k^{64}}$, $\mathbf{128^m}$, o^{256}, $\mathbf{512^q}$

The constant and variable alternate position between

the base and exponent. The variable skips every other letter of the alphabet (a, skip b, c, skip d, e, skip f, g, etc.). The constant is a power of 2: $2^1 = 2$, $2^2 = 4$, $2^3 = 8$, $2^4 = 16$, etc.

(10) 7, 2^3, 3^2, 2·5, 11, 2^2·3, 13, 2·7, 3·5, 2^4, **17**, **2·3²**, **19**, **2²·5**

These are the prime factors of every number: 7 is prime, 8 factors as $2 \times 2 \times 2$ (or 2^3), 9 factors as 3×3 (or 3^2), 10 factors as 2×5, 11 is prime, 12 factors as $2 \times 2 \times 3$ (or $2^2 \times 3$), 13 is prime, etc.

(11) $5x^2$, $7x^3$, $11x^5$, $19x^9$, $35x^{17}$, $67x^{33}$, $\mathbf{131x^{65}}$, $\mathbf{259x^{129}}$, $\mathbf{515x^{257}}$, $\mathbf{1027x^{513}}$

Double the previous exponent and subtract 1 to get the new exponent: $2 \times 2 - 1 = 3$, $3 \times 2 - 1 = 5$, $5 \times 2 - 1 = 9$, $9 \times 2 - 1 = 17$, etc. The coefficient is twice the exponent plus 1: $2 \times 2 + 1 = 5$, $3 \times 2 + 1 = 7$, $5 \times 2 + 1 = 11$, $9 \times 2 + 1 = 19$, etc.

(12) $3x^2$, x^5, $4x^3$, $2x^6$, $5x^4$, $3x^7$, $6x^5$, $\mathbf{4x^8}$, $\mathbf{7x^6}$, $\mathbf{5x^9}$, $\mathbf{8x^7}$

The coefficient equals the previous exponent minus 1: $2 - 1 = 1$, $5 - 1 = 4$, $3 - 1 = 2$, $6 - 1 = 5$, $4 - 1 = 3$, etc. The exponent equals the previous coefficient plus 2: $3 + 2 = 5$, $1 + 2 = 3$, $4 + 2 = 6$, $2 + 2 = 4$, $5 + 2 = 7$, etc.

(13) x, $2x^{1/2}$, $\dfrac{x^2}{2}$, $\dfrac{2x^{\frac{3}{2}}}{3}$, $\dfrac{x^5}{5}$, $\dfrac{2x^{\frac{5}{2}}}{5}$, $\dfrac{x^{10}}{10}$, $\dfrac{2x^{\frac{7}{2}}}{7}$, $\dfrac{x^{17}}{17}$, $\dfrac{2x^{\frac{9}{2}}}{9}$, $\dfrac{x^{26}}{26}$, $\dfrac{2x^{\frac{11}{2}}}{11}$, $\dfrac{x^{37}}{37}$, $\dfrac{2x^{\frac{13}{2}}}{13}$, $\dfrac{x^{50}}{50}$, $\dfrac{2x^{\frac{15}{2}}}{15}$, $\dfrac{x^{65}}{65}$

Two sequences are merged together. Get the powers of one sequence by adding 1, adding 3, adding 5, adding 7, etc.: $1 + 1 = 2$, $2 + 3 = 5$, $5 + 5 = 10$, $10 + 7 = 17$, $17 + 9 = 26$, $26 + 11 = 37$, $37 + 13 = 50$, etc. Get the powers

of the other sequence by adding 1: $\frac{1}{2} + 1 = \frac{3}{2}, \frac{3}{2} + 1$
$= \frac{5}{2}, \frac{5}{2} + 1 = \frac{7}{2}, \frac{7}{2} + 1 = \frac{9}{2}$, etc. In either case, the coefficient is the reciprocal of the exponent: $(1)^{-1} = 1$,
$\left(\frac{1}{2}\right)^{-1} = 2$, $(2)^{-1} = \frac{1}{2}$, $\left(\frac{3}{2}\right)^{-1} = \frac{2}{3}$, $(5)^{-1} = \frac{1}{5}$, $\left(\frac{5}{2}\right)^{-1} = \frac{2}{5}$,
$(10)^{-1} = \frac{1}{10}$, etc.

(14) $\frac{8x^{\frac{1}{8}}}{3}$, $2x^{1/4}$, $\frac{8x^{\frac{3}{8}}}{5}$, $\frac{4x^{\frac{1}{2}}}{3}$, $\frac{8x^{\frac{5}{8}}}{7}$, $x^{3/4}$, $\frac{8x^{\frac{7}{8}}}{9}$, $\frac{4x}{5}$, $\frac{8x^{9/8}}{11}$, $\frac{2x^{\frac{5}{4}}}{3}$, $\frac{8x^{\frac{11}{8}}}{13}$

Add $\frac{1}{8}$ to each power $(\frac{1}{8} + \frac{1}{8} = \frac{1}{4}, \frac{1}{4} + \frac{1}{8} = \frac{3}{8}, \frac{3}{8} + \frac{1}{8} = \frac{1}{2}, \frac{1}{2} +$
$\frac{1}{8} = \frac{5}{8}$, etc.). To get the coefficient, add $\frac{1}{4}$ to the power and
find its reciprocal. For example, $\frac{1}{8} + \frac{1}{4} = \frac{3}{8}$ and $\left(\frac{3}{8}\right)^{-1} = \frac{8}{3}$.

Similarly, $\frac{1}{4} + \frac{1}{4} = \frac{1}{2}$ and $\left(\frac{1}{2}\right)^{-1} = 2$.

(15) $2x + 1$, $x - 3$, $3x - 2$, $4x - 5$, $7x - 7$, $11x - 12$, $18x - 19$, $29x - 31$, $\mathbf{47x - 50}$, $\mathbf{76x - 81}$, $\mathbf{123x - 131}$, $\mathbf{199x - 212}$

Add consecutive expressions: $2x + 1 + x - 3 = 3x - 2, x - 3 + 3x - 2 = 4x - 5, 3x - 2 + 4x - 5 = 7x - 7$, etc.

(16) $x, y, x^2, xy, y^2, x^3, x^2y, xy^2, y^3, \mathbf{x^4, x^3y, x^2y^2, xy^3}$

These are the powers of the variable terms when you foil $(x + y)$ raised to an integer power. For example, $(x + y)^1 = x + y, (x + y)^2 = x^2 + 2xy + y^2$, and $(x + y)^3 = x^3 + 3x^2y + 3xy^2 + y^3$.

(17) $2x^5$, $7x^3$, $5x^{11}$, $15x^7$, $11x^{23}$, $27x^{13}$, $17x^{35}$, $\mathbf{39x^{19}, 23x^{47}, 59x^{29}, 31x^{63}}$

The coefficients and exponents are alternately prime numbers (see Chapter 8): 2, 3, 5, 7, 11, 13, etc. The other number (coefficient or exponent) is twice the prime number plus one ($2 \times 2 + 1 = 5$, $3 \times 2 + 1 = 7$, $5 \times 2 + 1 = 11$, $7 \times 2 + 1 = 15$, $11 \times 2 + 1 = 23$, etc.).

(18) $3x + 4 = x^2$, $3x = x^2 - 4$, $6x = 2x^2 - 8$, $6x - 4 = 2x^2 - 12$, $12x - 8 = 4x^2 - 24$, $12x - 12 = 4x^2 - 28$, $24x - 24 = 8x^2 - 56$, $24x - 28 = 8x^2 - 60$, $\mathbf{48x - 56 = 16x^2 - 120}$, $\mathbf{48x - 60 = 16x^2 - 124}$, $\mathbf{96x - 120 = 32x^2 - 248}$, $\mathbf{96x - 124 = 32x^2 - 252}$

Subtract 4 from both sides, multiply both sides by 2, subtract 4 from both sides, multiply by 2, repeating this pattern. For example:

$$3x + 4 = x^2$$

Subtract 4:

$$3x + 4 - 4 = x^2 - 4$$
$$3x = x^2 - 4$$

Multiply by 2:

$$2(3x) = 2(x^2 - 4)$$
$$6x = 2x^2 - 8$$

Subtract 4:

$$6x - 4 = 2x^2 - 8 - 4$$
$$6x - 4 = 2x^2 - 12$$

Multiply by 2:

$$2(6x - 4) = 2(2x^2 - 12)$$
$$12x - 8 = 4x^2 - 24$$

(19) x^3, $x^4 + 3x^3$, $x^5 + 4x^4 + 5x^3$, $x^6 + 5x^5 + 6x^4 + 11x^3$, $x^7 + 6x^6 + 7x^5 + 13x^4 + 20x^3$, $x^8 + 7x^7 + 8x^6 + 15x^5 + 23x^4 + 38x^3$, $\mathbf{x^9 + 8x^8 + 9x^7 + 17x^6 + 26x^5 + 43x^4 + 69x^3}$, $\mathbf{x^{10} + 9x^9 + 10x^8 + 19x^7 + 29x^6 + 48x^5 + 77x^4 + 125x^3}$

Raise the first power by 1 $(x^3, x^4, x^5$, etc.). The coefficient of the second term is 1 less than the power of the first term $(4 - 1 = 3, 5 - 1 = 4, 6 - 1 = 5$, etc.). The power of each term decreases by 1. For the third coefficients and onward, add the last 2 coefficients together (for example, with $x^7 + 6x^6 + 7x^5 + 13x^4 + 20x^3, 1 + 6 = 7, 6 + 7 = 13$, and $7 + 13 = 20$).

(20) 1, $x + y$, $x^2 + 2xy + y^2$, $x^3 + 3x^2y + 3xy^2 + y^3$, $x^4 + 4x^3y + 6x^2y^2 + 4xy^3 + y^4$, $x^5 + 5x^4y + 10x^3y^2 + 10x^2y^3 + 5xy^4 + y^5$, $x^6 + 6x^5y + 15x^4y^2 + 20x^3y^3 + 15x^2y^4 + 6xy^5 + y^6$, $\mathbf{x^7 + 7x^6y + 21x^5y^2 + 35x^4y^3 + 35x^3y^4 + 21x^2y^5 + 7xy^6 + y^7}$, $\mathbf{x^8 + 8x^7y + 28x^6y^2 + 56x^5y^3 + 70x^4y^4 + 56x^3y^5 + 28x^2y^6 + 8xy^7 + y^8}$

Multiply $(x + y)$ raised to an integer power. For example, $(x + y)^1 = x + y, (x + y)^2 = x^2 + 2xy + y^2$, and $(x + y)^3 = x^3 + 3x^2y + 3xy^2 + y^3$.

16 Visual

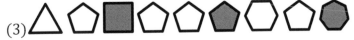

(1)
The center triangle is always black. A second triangle appears black on the left, right, top, left, right, top, etc.

(2)
Rotate counterclockwise 90°.

(3)

Two patterns are merged together: One is triangle, square, pentagon, hexagon, heptagon, etc., while the other is always a pentagon. Also, every third shape is gray.

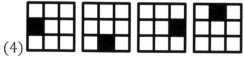

(4)

Rotate counterclockwise 90°.

(5)

Subtract the right number from the left number to get the top number: 5 – 2 = 3, 6 – 5 = 1, 11 – 7 = 4, and 13 – 5 = 8.

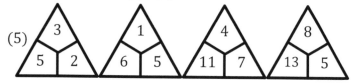

(6)

Copy the triangle and flip it upside down, joining this flipped triangle to the original to make the diamond. Do the same thing to the square to get the rectangle, and to the pentagon to find the answer.

(7)

Draw the top of a T, add the bottom of the T, add the top of a new smaller T to the right of the first one, add the bottom of this T, add the top of a third yet smaller T to the right of the previous T, etc.

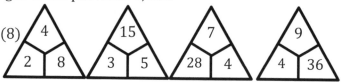

(8)

Multiply two numbers to get the third number. The third number appears at the right, then the top, then the left, then the right, etc.

(9)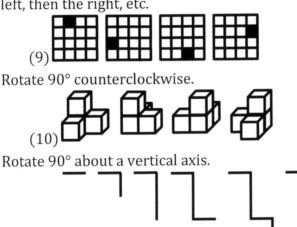

Rotate 90° counterclockwise.

(10)

Rotate 90° about a vertical axis.

(11)

Take one step right. Take one step down. Take a second step down. Take one step right. Take one step down. Take a second step down. Repeat this pattern.

(12)

Cut the width in half, cut the height in half, cut the width in half, cut the height in half, etc. Also, shade white, gray, black, white, gray, black, etc.

(13)

Rotate 90° about a horizontal axis.

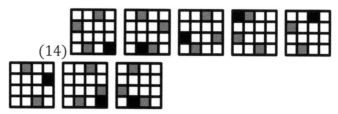

(14)

The black square advances 2 spaces along a clockwise direction. Ignoring the black square, the pattern flips horizontally, vertically, horizontally, vertically, and so on. If the black square coincides with a gray square (as in the fifth and sixth diagrams), the square appears black.

(15)

Black out the top row, then the middle row, then the bottom row, then the top row again, etc. The left column is blacked out for the first three, the middle column is blacked out for the second three, and the right column is blacked out for the next three (only 2 of these are shown).

3	4		2	8		1	9		5	6		7	9
5	7		7	9		3	6		10	20		13	50

(16)

Multiply the top numbers and subtract the bottom left number to get the bottom right number: $3 \times 4 - 5 = 7$, $1 \times 9 - 3 = 6$, $5 \times 6 - 10 = 20$, and $7 \times 9 - 13 = 50$.

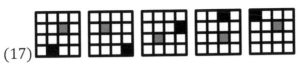

(17)

The black square advances 2 spaces along a clockwise path. The gray squares advances 1 space along a smaller clockwise path.

(18)

One arrow rotates 135° clockwise (↖,→,↙,↑,↘, and ←), while the other arrow rotates 90° counterclockwise (→,↑,←,↓,→, and ↑).

(19)

The vertical line of 3 squares remains constant. The fourth square moves along a counterclockwise path (down, down, over to the bottom, over to the bottom right, up, etc.).

(20)

Rotate the right half with the top coming forward, rotate the top half with the front going to the right, and repeat this pair of rotations over and over. (In the original cube, the left and right faces are black, the front and back faces are white, and the top and bottom faces are gray.)

17 Arrays

(1)

8	16	24
32	40	48
56	64	72

Multiples of 8 appear in order from left to right, top to bottom: $8 \times 1 = 8$, $8 \times 2 = 16$, $8 \times 3 = 24$, $8 \times 4 = 32$, $8 \times 5 = 40$, etc.

(2)

95	84	73
62	51	40
29	18	7

Subtract 11, working left to right, top to bottom: $95 - 11 = 84$, $84 - 11 = 73$, $73 - 11 = 62$, $62 - 11 = 51$, etc.

(3)

3	6	12
4	8	16
5	10	20

Double the left column to make the middle column ($3 \times 2 = 6$, $4 \times 2 = 8$, and $5 \times 2 = 10$). Double the middle column to make the right column ($6 \times 2 = 12$, $8 \times 2 = 16$, and $10 \times 2 = 20$).

(4)

2	7	17
3	11	19
5	13	23

Prime numbers (Chapter 8) are arranged top to bottom, left to right: 2, 3, 5, 7, 11, 13, 17, 19, and 23.

(5)

4	3	8
9	5	1
2	7	6

This is a magic square: The numbers of every row (4 + 3 + 8 = 15, 9 + 5 + 1 = 15, and 2 + 7 + 6 = 15), every column (4 + 9 + 2 = 15, 3 + 5 + 7 = 15, and 8 + 1 + 6 = 15), and every diagonal (4 + 5 + 6 = 15 and 2 + 5 + 8 = 15) add up to 15.

(6)

4	6	9	11
16	18	25	27
36	38	49	51
64	66	81	83

The first and third columns are perfect squares: $2^2 = 4$, $3^2 = 9$, $4^2 = 16$, $5^2 = 25$, $6^2 = 36$, etc. The second and fourth columns are 2 more than the previous columns. For example, 4 + 2 = 6, 9 + 2 = 11, 16 + 2 = 18, and 25 + 2 = 27.

(7)

●	●	♦	●
♦	●	●	♦
●	♦	●	●
♦	●	♦	●

The pattern ● ● ◆ ● ◆ repeats over and over from left to right, top to bottom.

(8)

14	17	19	20
10	13	16	18
7	9	12	15
5	6	8	11

The numbers 5 thru 20 appear in order (5, 6, 7, 8, 9, etc.). After 5, the next diagonal is 6 and 7, followed by 8, 9, and 10, etc.

(9)

1	1	0	0
2	8	7	14
3	27	26	52
4	64	63	126

The second column equals the first column cubed ($1^3 = 1$, $2^3 = 8$, $3^3 = 27$, and $4^3 = 64$). The third column is one less than the second column ($1 - 1 = 0$, $8 - 1 = 7$, $27 - 1 = 26$, and $64 - 1 = 63$). The last column is twice the third column ($0 \times 2 = 0$, $7 \times 2 = 14$, $26 \times 2 = 52$, and $63 \times 2 = 126$).

(10)

II	IV	VIII
XVI	XXXII	LXIV
CXXVIII	CCLVI	DXII

Powers of 2 appear in Roman numerals (Chapter 10): 2^1

$= 2$ (II), $2^2 = 4$ (IV), $2^3 = 8$ (VIII), $2^4 = 16$ (XVI), $2^5 = 32$ (XXXII), etc.

(11)

1	2	5	6
4	3	8	7
9	10	13	14
12	11	16	15

The numbers 1-16 appear in order. Divide the large 4×4 square into 4 smaller 2×2 squares. Write the numbers 1-4 in the top left 2×2 square in a clockwise fashion. Write the numbers 5-8 in the top right 2×2 square in a clockwise fashion. Write the numbers 9-12 in the bottom left 2×2 square in a clockwise fashion. Similarly, write the numbers 13-16 in the bottom right 2×2 square in a clockwise fashion.

(12)

2	3	5	9
2049	4097	8193	17
1025	32769	16385	33
513	257	129	65

Beginning with 2, multiply the previous number by 2 and subtract 1: $2 \times 2 - 1 = 3$, $3 \times 2 - 1 = 5$, $5 \times 2 - 1 = 9$, $9 \times 2 - 1 = 17$, $17 \times 2 - 1 = 33$, $33 \times 2 - 1 = 65$, etc. Write these numbers in a clockwise spiral from outside to inside.

(13)

5	8	■	14
17	■	23	26
■	32	35	■
41	44	■	50

Add 3 to each number, working left to right, top to bottom: $5 + 3 = 8, 8 + 3 = 11, 11 + 3 = 14, 14 + 3 = 17, 17 + 3 = 20$, etc. When a number coincides with a black square, simply don't write it (11, 20, 29, 38, and 47 are hidden by black squares).

(14)

1	2	3	4
2	3	5	7
3	5	8	12
4	8	13	20

Add the number directly above a cell to the number diagonally up and to the left of the cell. For example, $1 + 2 = 3, 2 + 3 = 5, 3 + 4 = 7, 3 + 5 = 8$, and $5 + 7 = 12$. This last example is illustrated below:

(15)

2	1	1
8	5	3
34	21	13

The Fibonacci sequence (Chapter 9) appears right to left, top to bottom: $1 + 1 = 2, 1 + 2 = 3, 2 + 3 = 5, 3 + 5 = 8, 5 + 8 = 13, 13 + 8 = 21$, and $13 + 21 = 34$.

18 Analogies

(1) three : 27 :: four : 64

(D) 64

Raise the first number to the third power: $3^3 = 27$ and $4^3 = 64$.

(2)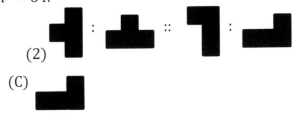

(C)

Rotate the first shape 90° clockwise.

(3) hand : wrist :: foot : ankle

(A) ankle

The wrist joins the hand to the arm, while the ankle joins the foot to the leg.

(4) 81 : 9 :: 36 : 6

(C) 6

Squareroot the first number: $\sqrt{81} = 9$ and $\sqrt{36} = 6$. (Take only the positive root.)

(5) century : year :: meter : centimeter

(A) centimeter

A century lasts 100 times longer than a year, while a meter is 100 times longer than a centimeter. (There are 100 years in one century, and 100 centimeters in one meter.)

(6) ADE : 145 :: CFH : 368

Answers

(C) 368
A is the 1st letter of the alphabet, D is the 4th letter, and E is the 5th letter. Put these together to make 145. Similarly, C is the 3rd letter, F is the 6th letter, and H is the 8th letter, which makes 368.

(7)

(C)

Flip the first image about a vertical axis: The second image is the reflection of the first. (Tip: hold this page up to a mirror.)

(8) moon : earth :: Venus : sun

(C) sun
The moon orbits the earth, while Venus orbits the sun.

(9) circle : circumference :: square : perimeter

(D) perimeter
The distance around a circle is its circumference, while the distance around a square is its perimeter.

(10) (3, 4, 5) : 35 :: (6, 7, 8) : 104

(D) 104
Add the first two numbers and multiply by the third: $(3 + 4) \times 5 = 7 \times 5 = 35$ and $(6 + 7) \times 8 = 13 \times 8 = 104$.

(11) uncle : nephew :: aunt : niece

(D) niece
Here is an example: John's brother is Kyle. Jane's sister is Kate. John and Jane get married, and have two kids, Luke and Lisa.

Kyle is Luke's uncle; Luke is Kyle's nephew. Kate is Lisa's aunt; Lisa is Kate's niece.

(Luke's uncle is his father's brother; Kyle's nephew is his brother's son. Lisa's aunt is her mother's sister; Kate's niece is her sister's daughter.)

(12) (10, 11) : 101 :: (100, 101) : 1001

(C) 1001

The binary numbers 10 and 11 are the numbers 2 and 3 in the decimal system. Add 2 and 3 to make 5, which is 101 in binary. The binary numbers 100 and 101 equate to 4 and 5 in decimal form. Add 4 and 5 to make 9, which is 1001 in binary.

Note: Binary numbers are made of 0's and 1's. The following table shows the relationship between decimal numbers and binary numbers:

Decimal	Binary
1	1
2	10
3	11
4	100
5	101
6	110
7	111
8	1000
9	1001
10	1010

(13) horse : foal :: deer : fawn

(C) fawn

A baby horse is called a foal, while a baby deer is called

a fawn.

(14) rectangle : square :: parallelogram : rhombus

(C) rhombus

If you make the sides of a rectangle have equal length, you get a square. Similarly, if you make the sides of a parallelogram have equal length, you get a rhombus.

(15) $\frac{5}{8} : 1\frac{1}{4} :: \frac{3}{4} : 1\frac{1}{2}$

(B) $1\frac{1}{2}$

Double the first number: $5/8 \times 2 = 10/8 = 5/4 = 1 + 1/4$ and $3/4 \times 2 = 6/4 = 3/2 = 1 + 1/2$.

(16)

(A)

Rotate the right half with the top coming to the front, then rotate the bottom half with the front going to the right. (The simpler solution is to change white to black, gray to white, and black to gray.)

(17) $\left(8, \frac{2}{3}\right) : 4 :: \left(81, \frac{3}{4}\right) : 27$

(D) 27

Raise the first number to the power of the fraction: $(8)^{2/3} = 4$ and $(81)^{3/4} = 27$. (Take the positive root in the latter case.)

(18) COCCOON : C_3O_3N :: COCOA : C_2O_2A

(B) C_2O_2A

The word COCCOON has 3 C's, 3 O's, and 1 N, forming C_3O_3N. The word COCOA has 2 C's, 2 O's, and 1 A, forming C_2O_2A. (These are not chemical formulas, even though they might resemble such.)

(19) circle : sphere : : square : cube

(A) cube

Here is one way to look at this: If you slice a sphere down the middle, you obtain a circular cross section. If you slice a cube down the middle parallel to one face, you obtain a square cross section.

(20) PUZZLES : OTYYKDR :: PATTERNS : OZSSDQMR

(A) OZSSDQMR

Replace each letter with the letter that comes before it in the alphabet. For example, replace B with A, replace C with B, and replace D with C. Also, replace A with Z.

In the word PATTERNS, P becomes O, A becomes Z, the T's become S's, the E becomes D, the R becomes Q, the N becomes M, and the S becomes R, forming OZSSDQMR. (This is a cryptogram.)

About the Author

Chris McMullen is a physics instructor at Northwestern State University of Louisiana and also an author of academic books. Whether in the classroom or as a writer, Dr. McMullen loves sharing knowledge and the art of motivating and engaging students.

He earned his Ph.D. in phenomenological high-energy physics (particle physics) from Oklahoma State University in 2002. Originally from California, Dr. McMullen earned his Master's degree from California State University, Northridge, where his thesis was in the field of electron spin resonance.

As a physics teacher, Dr. McMullen observed that many students lack fluency in fundamental math skills. In an effort to help students of all ages and levels master basic math skills, he published a series of math workbooks on arithmetic, fractions, and algebra called the Improve Your Math Fluency Series. Dr. McMullen has also published a variety of science books, including introductions to basic astronomy and chemistry concepts in addition to physics textbooks.

Dr. McMullen is very passionate about teaching. Many students and observers have been impressed with the transformation that occurs when he walks into the classroom, and the interactive engaged discussions that he leads during class time. Dr. McMullen is well-known for drawing monkeys and using them in his physics examples and problems, using his creativity to inspire students. A stressed out student is likely to be told to throw some bananas at monkeys, smile, and think happy physics thoughts.

Improve Your Math Fluency

This series of math workbooks is geared toward
practicing essential math skills:

- Algebra and trigonometry
- Fractions, decimals, and percentages
- Long division
- Multiplication and division
- Addition and subtraction

Science Books

Dr. McMullen has published a variety of science books,
including:

- Basic astronomy concepts
- Basic chemistry concepts
- Creative physics problems
- Calculus-based physics

Puzzle Books

Chris McMullen enjoys solving puzzles. His favorite puzzle is Kakuro (kind of like a cross between crossword puzzles and Sudoku). He once taught a three-week summer course on puzzles.

In addition to the pattern puzzle book that you are reading right now, Chris McMullen has coauthored several word scramble books.

This includes a cool idea called VErBAl ReAcTiONS. A VErBAl ReAcTiON expresses word scrambles so that they look like chemical reactions. Here is an example:

$$2\,C + U + 2\,S + Es \rightarrow S\,U\,C\,C\,Es\,S$$

The left side of the reaction indicates that the answer has 2 C's, 1 U, 2 S's, and 1 Es. Rearrange CCUSSEs to form SUCCEsS.

Each answer is not merely a word, it's a chemical word. A chemical word is made up not of letters, but of elements of the periodic table. In this case, SUCCEsS is made up of sulfur (S), uranium (U), carbon (C), and Einsteinium (Es).

Another example of a chemical word is GeNiUS. It's made up of germanium (Ge), nickel (Ni), uranium (U), and sulfur (S).

If you enjoy anagrams and like science or math, these puzzles are tailor-made for you.

Made in the USA
San Bernardino, CA
31 July 2019